bag STYLE

20 Inspirational handbags, totes, and carry-alls to knit and crochet

bag STYLE

20 Inspirational handbags, totes, and carry-alls to knit and crochet

PAM ALLEN & ANN BUDD

INTERWEAVE.
interweavestore.com

PHOTOGRAPHY: **Carol Kaplan**

COVER AND INTERIOR DESIGN: **Jillfrances Gray**

TECHNICAL EDITING: **Karen Frisa**

Interweave Press LLC
201 East Fourth Street
Loveland, CO 80537-5655 USA
interweavestore.com

Printed in China by Asia Pacific Offset

Library of Congress Cataloging-in-Publication Data

Allen, Pam, 1949-
  Bag Style : 20 Inspriational hangbags, totes, and carry-
alls to knit and crochet / Pam Allen and Ann Budd, authors.
    p. cm.
  Includes bibliographical references and index.
   ISBN 978-1-59668-028-9 (pbk.)
  1. Knitted bag—Patterns. I. Budd, Ann, 1956- II. Title.
  TT805.K54A44 2007
  746.43'2041—dc22

                                          2006031041

10 9 8 7 6 5 4 3

ACKNOWLEDGMENTS

Once again, we're fortunate to work with many talented people who help make the Style series successful. For their imaginative bag projects, we thank the designers: Véronik Avery, Lisa Daehlin, Mary D'Alton, Bri Ana Drennon, Joshua Eckels, Lisa B. Evans, Norah Gaughan, Regina Rioux Gonzales, Katie Himmelberg, Laura Irwin, Kate Jackson, Mags Kandis, Mary Jane Mucklestone, Kristin Nicholas, Ruthie Nussbaum, Sharon O'Brien, Theresa Schabes, and Judith L. Swartz.

We're grateful to our technical editor, Karen Frisa, for her clear and concise project patterns, and to our copy editor, Veronica Patterson, for fine-tuning our text.

As in the previous books in this series, we thank Jillfrances Gray for her good-looking book design; Carol Kaplan for her engaging photographs; photo assistant Denise LeBreux, stylist Carrie Hoge, and models Stacey Collins, Maureen Emerson, Megan Heavenor, Melisande Lopez, and Tonye Masse.

Finally, we are indebted to Denise Novotny and Missy Tasker at Simply Chic (shop simplychic.com) and Angie Bibeau at Bliss (blissboutique.com) in Portland, Maine, for their generosity in lending us garments for styling. Also, warmest thanks to the people who provided locations: Nancy Grayson at Cunningham Books, Virginia Sassman and Andres Verzosa at Aucosisco Gallery, Gerrie Brooke at Portland Roasting Company, Melora Gregory at Portland Yoga Studio, Oliver Keithly and the folks at Porthole Café, and John Walsh at Arabica Café—all in Portland, Maine.

CONTENTS

WHY BAGS?

Even though we weren't there to see it, we're willing to bet that the first bag was invented sometime in prehistory when cavemen and women scavenged the countryside for food and had the good fortune to find more than they could carry. Since then, bags have become a necessity of life for carrying and storing all of our stuff. In addition to the all-purpose home-away-from-home handbag we grab before heading out the door, we need book bags, garment bags, cosmetic bags, grocery bags, soccer bags, lunch bags, even garbage bags. And let's not forget about a bag for our knitting projects. That's a lot of bags!

No wonder we think about bags so much, and no wonder they're a favorite project among knitters and crocheters. In addition to being useful, bags are relatively quick to knit, turn out well even if your gauge is off, and offer countless creative possibilities in their design.

Following the format of the popular Style series (*Scarf Style*, *Wrap Style*, *Lace Style*, and *Folk Style*), *Bag Style* is a book of projects to knit as well as a book about knitting bags. It's a collection of patterns for handbags and more that range from small to large and from simple to not-so-simple. Each bag offers an individual lesson in inspiration, technique, application, and, of course, style. As a collection, the patterns will give you new ways to think about knitted and crocheted bags and provide you with ideas and inspiration for your own inventions.

After you've taken in the twenty projects, turn to the Design Notebook (page 100), where you'll find a discussion of the elements of knitted and crocheted bags and how to combine these elements into your own designs. You'll learn how to give a bag shape, depth, stability, handles, and closures, and you'll gain ideas for adding different kinds of embellishment.

Don't worry if you've never made your own bag before. At the end of the book, you'll find a glossary of terms and techniques that includes illustrated instructions for all the specific techniques mentioned in the projects. Along with the easy-to-follow directions and clear illustrations in the project and design chapters, the glossary will provide the help you need to successfully complete any project in this book.

Bags have become a necessity of life for carrying and storing all of our stuff.

bagPATTERNS

ZENITH CARPET BAG
VÉRONIK AVERY

Véronik Avery designed this uptown bag to be large enough to hold a few books or important files and chic enough to wear with a business suit and heels. The front and back of the bag are identical, beginning with a narrow base, followed by stitches cast on for the side gusset, and ending with a contrasting horizontal band at the top. For stability (and to keep pens and pencils from slipping out), Véronik added a contrasting lining. The bag fastens with a snap-frame closure that holds the upper edges securely. For versatility, Véronik attached a pair of short leather handles as well as a shoulder strap.

BACK

CO 90 sts. *Set-up row:* (WS) P1 (selvedge st; work in St st throughout), work Row 1 of Cable chart over next 88 sts, p1 (selvedge st; work in St st throughout). Working selvedge sts in St st, cont in patt until piece measures 1¾" (4.5 cm) from CO.

Make Sides

Using the backward-loop method (see Glossary, page 119), CO 12 sts at end of next 2 rows, working newly CO sts in patt and new selvedge sts in St st—114 sts.
Cont even in patt until piece measures 16" (40.5 cm) from CO, ending with a WS row.
Next row: K1, *k2tog; rep from * to last st, k1—58 sts rem. BO all sts.

FRONT

Work same as back.

TOP BAND (make 2)

CO 20 sts.
Row 1 and all WS rows: K2, p2, k1, p10, k1, p2, k2.
Rows 2 and 4: K2, RT (see chart key), k12, RT, k2.
Row 6: K2, RT, k1, sl 5 sts to cn and hold in back, k5, k5 from cn, k1, RT, k2.
Rows 8, 10, and 12: Rep Row 2.
Rep Rows 1–12 eight more times—band measures about 16" (40.5 cm) from CO. BO all sts.

FINISHED SIZE
About 15" (38 cm) wide, 19" (48.5 cm) tall, and 4" (10 cm) deep, excluding handles.

YARN
Chunky weight (#5 Bulky).

Shown here: Reynolds Rapture (50% wool, 50% silk; 72 yd [66 m]/50 g): #710 dark teal, 12 balls.

NEEDLES
Size 6 (4 mm): 24" (60 cm) circular (cir). Adjust needle size if necessary to obtain the correct gauge.

NOTIONS
Cable needle (cn); marker (m); tapestry needle; 16" (40.5 cm) snap frame (item #LV77 from www.lacis.com); 15" x 39" (38 x 99 cm) fabric for lining; sharp-point sewing needles for each thread weight; thread to match lining fabric; buttonhole twist thread to match straps and handle; two 19" (48.5 cm) leather handles; 32" (81.5 cm) leather strap.

GAUGE
24 stitches and 32 rows = 4" (10 cm) in charted cable pattern.

Can't decide
between traditional
leather handles and
a shoulder strap?
Use both!

Cable

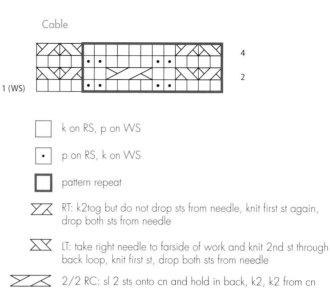

1 (WS)

4

2

- ☐ k on RS, p on WS
- ▪ p on RS, k on WS
- ☐ pattern repeat
- RT: k2tog but do not drop sts from needle, knit first st again, drop both sts from needle
- LT: take right needle to farside of work and knit 2nd st through back loop, knit first st, drop both sts from needle
- 2/2 RC: sl 2 sts onto cn and hold in back, k2, k2 from cn

FINISHING

With yarn threaded on a tapestry needle, sew CO edge of side to selvedge edge of bottom of each bag piece as shown below. Sew top band to front and back pieces, positioning garter edges on top so they overlap and conceal BO row. Using the mattress st (see Glossary, page 124), sew front to back along sides. Weave in loose ends.

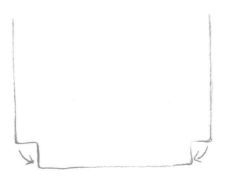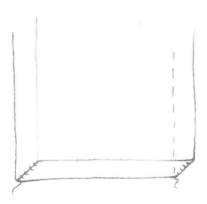

Sew CO edge of side to selvedge edge of bottom.

Facing

With WS facing and holding bag upside
down, pick up and knit 72 sts along each top
band, 2 sts in from the edge—144 sts. Place
marker (pm) and join for working in the rnd.
Work in St st until facing measures 2½" (6.5 cm)
from pick-up row. Loosely BO all sts. Turn bag
inside out and position snap frame between
top band and facing and, with yarn threaded
on a tapestry needle, sew BO edge of facing to
top edge of bag, enclosing snap frame in
the process.

Lining

With RS tog, sew shorter sides of lining fabric
tog to form a tube. Sew tube closed at one
end. Bring side and bottom seam tog, forming a
triangular point at bottom and sew a perpendic-
ular seam 2" (5 cm) down from point of triangle.
Repeat on other side. Turn lining RS out. Fold
top edge down ½" (1.3 cm) to WS and press.
Insert bag inside lining, thereby concealing WS
and use a whipstitch (see Glossary, page 124)
to sew top of lining to bottom of facing.

With buttonhole twist threaded on a sewing
needle, sew handles to RS of bag, 3" (7.5 cm)
from top edge. Sew ends of strap to side
seams, 1" (2.5 cm) below bottom of top band.

Mary D'Alton turned to Japanese origami for the construction of this clever bag. She knitted two diamonds—one burgundy and one chartreuse—then folded them together into a triangle shape. She made the handles by working the last three stitches of two of the diamonds into a long piece of I-cord, which she sewed to the top edge of the opposite diamond. To keep the construction simple, Mary felted the whole thing to firm up the knitted fabric, making a sturdy pouch-style bag—no need for a lining; no need for a closure.

FIRST HALF

With burgundy, CO 3 sts. Work in St st for 2 rows. Inc as foll:

Row 1: (RS) Knit.

Row 2: Purl.

Row 3: K1, M1R (see Glossary, page 123), knit to end—1 st inc'd.

Row 4: Purl.

Row 5: K1, M1R, knit to last st, M1L (see Glossary, page 123), k1—2 sts inc'd.

Row 6: Purl.

Rep Rows 3–6 seven more times—27 sts. Work Rows 1 and 2 once, then work Rows 3–6 three times—36 sts. Rep the last 14 rows 4 more times—72 sts. Work Rows 3–6 once, then work Rows 3 and 4 once more—76 sts. Rep Rows 1 and 2 three times for bottom edge of bag. Dec as foll:

Row 7: K1, k2tog, knit to end of row—1 st dec'd.

Row 8: Purl.

Row 9: K1, k2tog, knit to last 3 sts, ssk, k1—2 sts dec'd.

Row 10: Purl.

Work Rows 7 and 8 once more—72 sts rem. Work Rows 1 and 2 once, then work Rows 7–10 three times—63 sts rem. Rep the last 14 rows 4 more times—27 sts rem. Work Rows 7–10 eight times—3 sts rem. Work Rows 1 and 2 two times.

Handle

Change to dpn and work 3-st I-cord (see Glossary, page 124) until handle measures 25" (63.5 cm). BO all sts.

FINISHED SIZE

About 18" (45.5 cm) wide at base and 11" (28 cm) tall after felting, excluding handles.

YARN

Worsted weight (#4 Medium).

Shown here: Harrisville Designs New England Highland (100% wool; 200 yd [183 m]/100 g): #39 russet (burgundy) and #07 tundra (chartreuse), 1 ball each.

NEEDLES

Size 6 (4 mm): straight and set of 2 double-pointed (dpn). Adjust needle size if necessary to obtain the correct gauge.

NOTIONS

Tapestry needle; net laundry bag.

GAUGE

18 stitches and 26 rows = 4" (10 cm) in stockinette stitch, before felting. *Note:* Swatch both colors of yarn to make sure they have the same gauge.

A bit of origami
makes a smart purse.

SECOND HALF

With chartreuse, CO 3 sts and work as for first half.

FINISHING

Block pieces so that they are exactly the same size.

Assembly

Overlap the pieces so that the burgundy piece is on top of the chartreuse piece. With burgundy threaded on a tapestry needle, sew the pieces tog as invisibly as possible. On the WS of the bag, sew along the bag base (where it will be folded) to secure the two layers tog. Fold the bag in half with RS tog and sew side seams from the bottom corner until even with the base of the V in the center front and back of the bag. Weave in loose ends. Turn bag RS out.

Felting

Place bag in net laundry bag and run through washer cycle set on small load, hot wash, and cold rinse, adding a small amount of mild detergent. Stop the washer periodically to check the progress of the felting; run through additional cycles if necessary to achieve the desired amount of felting (no stitches should be visible).

Attach Handles

Attach burgundy handle to top of chartreuse point on one side of bag and attach chartreuse handle to top of burgundy point on other side of bag. To attach handle, position end of handle behind point and, using yarn color to match point of bag, whipstitch (see Glossary, page 124) in place.

Dense felted stitches can produce a fabric that's nearly as sturdy as leather.

While vacationing in the Caribbean, Mags Kandis purchased a souvenir backpack made of palm leaves that was, although beautiful to look at, scratchy to wear. So, she copied the narrow elongated shape in a soft wool yarn in the festive colors of ocean-side cabanas and bright beach towels. She worked the body side to side for vertical stripes and placed eyelet holes along the opening edge for a drawstring. She knitted a separate piece for the foldover flap and embellished it with felted crochet circles. Mags shaped the bottom of the bag with sewn gussets and knitted the straps in narrow strips of stockinette stitch that roll in on themselves naturally.

NOTE
✦ Body of backpack is knitted sideways for ease of color changes.

STITCH GUIDE

Drawstring Eyelet Pattern
Rows 1–8 and 10–14: Work in St st.
Rows 9 and 15: (RS) Knit to last 6 sts, k2tog, yo, k4.
Rows 16–22: Work in St st.
Repeat Rows 1–22 for pattern.

FINISHED SIZE
About 14¾" (37.5 cm) wide, 20" (51 cm) tall, and 4½" deep before felting; 8½" (21.5 cm) wide, 18" (45.5 cm) tall, and 3" (7.5 cm) deep after felting.

YARN
Worsted weight (#4 Medium).

Shown here: Vermont Organic Fiber Company O-Wool (100% wool; 198 yd [181 m]/100 g): #440 sumac (red; A), #5401 garnet (wine; B), 2 skeins each; #6402 saffron (gold; C), 1 skein.

NEEDLES
Size 10½ (6.5 mm). Adjust needle size if necessary to obtain the correct gauge.

NOTIONS
Size K/10½ (6.5 mm) crochet hook; tapestry needle; net laundry bag.

GAUGE
13 stitches and 20 rows = 4" (10 cm) in stockinette stitch before felting.

Hide a drawstring
closure under a
decorative flap.

BODY

With B, CO 72 sts. Work 10 rows in St st. Change to C and work 2 rows in St st. Change to A and work Rows 1–22 of drawstring eyelet patt (see Stitch Guide). Change to C and work 2 rows in St st. Change to B and work Rows 1–22 of drawstring eyelet patt. Change to C and work 2 rows in St st. Change to A and work Rows 1–22 of drawstring eyelet patt. Change to C and work 2 rows in St st. Change to B and work 22 rows in St st. Change to C and work 2 rows in St st. Change to A and work Rows 1–22 of drawstring eyelet patt. Change to C and work 2 rows in St st. Change to B and work Rows 1–22 of drawstring eyelet patt. Change to C and work 2 rows in St st. Change to A and work Rows 1–22 of drawstring eyelet patt. Change to C and work 2 rows in St st. Change to B and work 12 rows in St st—192 rows total. BO all sts.

FLAP

With C, CO 26 sts. Work in St st for 52 rows. BO all sts.

STRAP

With B, CO 5 sts. Work in St st until piece measures 95" (241.5 cm) from CO. BO all sts.

DRAWSTRING

With C, CO 3 sts. Work in St st until piece measures 54" (137 cm) from CO. BO all sts.

FINISHING

Weave in loose ends.

Seams

With B threaded on a tapestry needle, sew CO edge to BO edge of body. With RS tog, fold bag so that panels of B without drawstring holes line up (the back will be the panel of B with the seam) and sew tog to form base of backpack. With bag inside out, flatten bag bottom so that the middle of the base seam is centered and faces up (see Design Notebook, pages 106–107). With B, sew a seam across each corner to form "ears." Fold "ears" toward center of bag base and lightly sew in place.

Flap Embellishment

Small Circles: (make 2 with A; 1 with B) With crochet hook, ch 22, sl st into first ch to form ring. Fasten off. Cut yarn, leaving a 16" (40.5 cm) tail to attach to flap later.

Large Circles (make 2 with B; 1 with A) With crochet hook, ch 30, sl st into first ch to form ring. Fasten off. Cut yarn, leaving a 16" (40.5 cm) tail.

Using photo as a guide, use tails to secure crocheted circles onto flap. Keep in mind that the flap will shrink more in length than width during the felting process. To have finished circles appear more round, attach to flap in long oval shapes.

Felting

Place all pieces in a net laundry bag and run through washer cycle set for small load, hot wash, and cold rinse, and add a small amount of mild detergent. Stop the washer periodically to check the progress of the felting, and run additional cycles if necessary to achieve the desired amount of felting. When pieces are felted, remove from washer, pull into shape, and lay flat to air-dry.

Assembly

With C threaded on a tapestry needle, use the backstitch (see Glossary, page 124) to attach flap to back of backpack, centered between drawstring holes. Cut drawstring in half and knot cut end of each piece. Beg at flap, thread unknotted ends of drawstring through eyelets toward front. Knot and trim ends.

Fold strap in half and with C threaded on a tapestry needle, use backstitches to attach center of strap securely to backpack back centered below flap as shown below. Adjust for fit and knot straps at desired length in relation to bottom of backpack. With C threaded on a tapestry needle, attach straps above knots securely at bottom corners of backpack. Knot and trim ends.

Knit narrow stockinette-stitch strips and let them roll on themselves to form rounded straps.

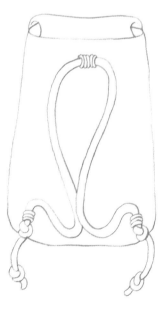

Attach straps to bag back with backstitches (flap not shown).

KNITTING NEEDLE KNITTING BAG
PAM ALLEN

Pam Allen indulged her fondness for the berry stitch in this quick-and-easy knitting bag whose cigar shape was inspired by a bag she saw in a catalog. For the front and back, she knitted two slightly shaped rectangles and seamed them along the bottom and partway up the sides. Rather than binding off, she placed the live stitches on wooden knitting needles, squished them together to form soft gathers, and applied a little superglue. Garter-stitch handles sewn to the front and back are all that's needed to finish the bag. This particular bag isn't lined, but it would be an easy matter to use the front and back as pattern pieces and add a cheery print lining to prevent needles from poking through.

BACK

With larger needles, CO 80 sts.
Row 1: (WS) K2, *(k1, p1, k1) in next st, p3tog; rep from * to last 2 sts, k2.
Row 2: Purl.
Row 3: K2, *p3tog, (k1, p1, k1) in next st; rep from * to last 2 sts, k2.
Row 4: Purl.
Rep Rows 1–4 until piece measures 9" (23 cm) from CO, ending with Row 4 of patt. *Dec row:* (WS) K2, *k1, p3tog; rep from * to last 2 sts, k2—42 sts rem. Loosely knit 1 row. With size 15 wooden needles, purl 1 row. Leave sts on needle.

FRONT

CO 80 sts and work as for back.

HANDLES (make 2)

With smaller needles, CO 6 sts. Work in garter st (knit every row) until piece measures 21" (53.5 cm) from CO. BO all sts.

FINISHING

Gently steam-press pieces. With yarn threaded on a tapestry needle, sew bottom seam. Beg at bottom edge, sew side seams for 5" (12.5 cm). Spread sts evenly along wooden needle from knob end to 1½" (3.8 cm) from tip. Use superglue to secure last few sts at pointed end. Sew handles to bag 10 sts in from each end.

FINISHED SIZE
About 18¾" (47.5 cm) wide and 9" (23 cm) tall, excluding handles.

YARN
Chunky weight (#5 Bulky).
Shown here: Nashua Handknits Creative Focus Chunky (75% wool, 25% alpaca; 110 yd [101 m]/100 g): #1940 dried rose, 3 balls.

NEEDLES
Bag—size 10½ (6.5 mm). Handles—size 9 (5.5 mm). Adjust needle size if necessary to obtain the correct gauge.

NOTIONS
Tapestry needle; size 15 (10 mm) wooden needles; superglue.

GAUGE
17 stitches and 19 rows = 4" (10 cm) in pattern stitch on larger needles.

Carry your important files and papers comfortably in Joshua Eckels's manly messenger bag. Joshua knitted five separate pieces for the bag—a front, back, flap, gusset, and shoulder pad. He felted them down to a dense, indestructible fabric in his washing machine, trimmed them square, then sewed them together. Under the foldover flap, Joshua added a heavy-duty zipper to keep the contents secure. The gusset gives the bag depth and provides a handy channel for the heavy nylon-webbing strap. Joshua added buckles to give the strap an adjustable fit, and he added a soft pad at the shoulder for comfort.

BACK

With MC, CO 101 sts. Work in St st until piece measures 17" (43 cm) from CO, ending with a WS row. [Dec 1 st each end of needle on next row. Work 3 rows even.] 2 times—97 sts rem. Dec 1 st each end of needle on next 3 rows—91 sts rem. Purl 1 (WS) row. *Next row:* K1, sssk (see Glossary, page 121), knit to last 4 sts, k3tog, k1—87 sts rem. BO all sts.

FRONT

With MC, CO 101 sts and work as for back.

FINISHED SIZE
About 16" (40.5 cm) wide, 11" (28 cm) tall, and 2½" (6.5 cm) deep after felting.

YARN
Worsted weight (#4 Medium).

Shown here: Plymouth Galway Highland Heather (100% wool; 210 yd [192 m]/100 g): #704 gray (MC), 4 balls; #710 burgundy (CC), 3 balls.

NEEDLES
Size 8 (5 mm): straight and set of 4 double-pointed (dpn). Adjust needle size if necessary to obtain the correct gauge.

NOTIONS
Marker (m); tapestry needle; sharp-point upholstery needle with large eye; 2 yd (2 m) 2" (5 cm) heavy nylon webbing for strap (available from fabric stores); 18" (45.5 cm) heavy-duty zipper; sewing thread to match zipper; two 2" (5 cm) single bar slide adjustable buckles.

GAUGE
20 stitches and 26 rows = 4" (10 cm) in stockinette stitch before felting; 24 stitches and 44 rows = 4" (10 cm) after felting.

FLAP

With MC, CO 101 sts. Work in St st until piece measures 18" (45.5 cm) from CO, ending with a WS row. Cont in short-rows (see Glossary, page 125) as foll:

Row 1: Knit to last 4 sts, wrap next st, turn.

Row 2: Purl to last 4 sts, wrap next st, turn.

Row 3: Knit to last 8 sts, wrap next st, turn.

Row 4: Purl to last 8 sts, wrap next st, turn.

Cont in this manner, working 4 fewer sts each row before wrapping and turning until 24 sts rem unworked at each end of needle, ending with a WS row. *Next row:* (RS) Knit, working the wraps tog with the wrapped sts. *Next row:* (WS) Purl, working the rem wraps tog with the wrapped sts. Change to CC and work even in St st until piece measures 2½" (6.5 cm) from color change, ending with a WS row. Dec 1 st each end of needle every RS row 4 times—93 sts rem. Purl 1 WS row. *Next row:* (RS) K1, sssk, knit to last 4 sts, k3tog, k1—4 sts dec'd. Purl 1 WS row. Rep the last 2 rows once more—85 sts rem. BO 10 sts at beg of next 6 rows—25 sts rem. BO all sts.

GUSSET PANEL

With CC, CO 28 sts. Divide sts on 3 dpn so that there are 12 sts on Needle 1, 8 sts on Needle 2, and 8 sts on Needle 3. Place marker (pm) and join for working in the rnd, being careful not to twist sts. Knit 12 rnds.

Inc Rnd 1: [K13, k1f&b] 2 times—30 sts.

Knit 2 rnds even.

Inc Rnd 2: [K14, k1f&b] 2 times—32 sts.

Knit 2 rnds even.

Inc Rnd 3: [K15, k1f&b] 2 times—34 sts.

Knit 2 rnds even.

Inc Rnd 4: [K16, k1f&b] 2 times—36 sts.

Knit 2 rnds even.

Inc Rnd 5: [K17, k1f&b] 2 times—38 sts.

Knit 2 rnds even.

Inc Rnd 6: [K18, k1f&b] 2 times—40 sts.

Knit 22 rnds even.

The messenger bag is an ergonomic alternative to the traditional briefcase.

Strap Slit

Rnd 1: K14, BO 12 sts, knit to end.

Rnd 2: K14, use the backward-loop method (see Glossary, page 119) to CO 12 sts, knit to end. Knit 44 rnds. Rep Rnds 1 and 2 for 2nd slit. Knit 55 rnds. Rep Rnds 1 and 2 for 3rd slit. Knit 62 rnds. Rep Rnds 1 and 2 for 4th slit. Knit 55 rnds. Rep Rnds 1 and 2 for 5th slit. Knit 44 rnds. Rep Rnds 1 and 2 for 6th slit. Knit 22 rnds.

Dec Rnd 1: [K18, k2tog] 2 times—38 sts rem.

Knit 2 rnds even.

Dec Rnd 2: [K17, k2tog] 2 times—36 sts rem.

Knit 2 rnds even.

Dec Rnd 3: [K16, k2tog] 2 times—34 sts rem.

Knit 2 rnds even.

Dec Rnd 4: [K15, k2tog] 2 times—32 sts rem.

Knit 2 rnds even.

Dec Rnd 5: [K14, k2tog] 2 times—30 sts rem.

Knit 2 rnds even.

Dec Rnd 6: [K13, k2tog] 2 times—28 sts rem.

Knit 12 rnds—piece measures about 57" (145 cm) from CO. BO all sts.

SHOULDER PAD

With CC, CO 36 sts. Divide sts evenly on 3 dpn, pm, and join for working in the rnd, being careful not to twist sts. Knit 9 rnds. BO all sts.

Shoulder Pad Slit

Rnd 1: K12, BO 12 sts, knit to end.

Rnd 2: K12, use the backward-loop method to CO 12 sts, knit to end. Knit 26 rnds. Rep Rnds 1 and 2 for second slit. Knit 9 rnds.

ZIPPER BANDS (MAKE 2)

With MC, CO 101 sts. Work in St st for 16 rows. BO all sts.

FINISHING

Weave in loose ends.

Felting

Place pieces in washing machine on the lowest water level and hottest water setting with a normal amount of laundry soap (and a pair of blue jeans to improve agitation, if desired). Run through several agitation cycles. Check the pieces periodically for size and density. When the pieces are near the final size, remove from washing machine and cont to felt by hand as foll:

Fill a wash tub or basin with 2" (5 cm) of very hot water and a generous amount of laundry or dish soap. Wearing rubber gloves to protect your hands from the hot water, vigorously rub the pieces to saturate them with soapy water. Stop occasionally to check size and reshape. When the desired size and density has been reached, rinse out the soap while agitating under hot water. Cont to agitate while rinsing with cold water, making sure to remove all soap. Squeeze out as much water as possible, then roll in a bath towel to remove excess water.

Blocking

While still damp, lay pieces out flat on a towel and pull into shape (pin them temporarily if necessary). Make sure that front and back are identical and have one long straight edge and two rounded corners. The long straight edge of the flap should match those of the front and back. The slits on the gusset panel should be aligned and symmetrical. The zipper bands should be at least as long as the long straight edges of the front and back. Allow all pieces to thoroughly air-dry. If necessary, trim dry pieces with scissors.

ASSEMBLY

Attach Flap

Align back and flap face up along their long straight edges. Overlap these edges by about ¼" (6 mm), with the WS of the flap overlapping the RS of the back. With yarn (MC for invisible seam; CC for contrasting seam) threaded on a sharp needle, sew tog with a backstitch (see Glossary, page 124).

Attach Gusset Panel

Fold gusset in half to find center point. Beg at center bottom of bag and working to top edge, sew gusset to bag back using a ¼" (6 mm) seam allowance, matching center point of gusset to center bottom of bag. Make sure that slits on gusset are facing outside of bag, and that gusset extends beyond top of bag by an equal amount on each end. Sew extra reinforcing stitches at top of bag. Sew gusset to front of bag in same manner.

Zipper Bands

Lay out zipper bands with two long edges tog. Place zipper on top of bands, wrong side up. Pin in place and, using a sewing needle and matching thread, sew both sides of the zipper to band. If the zipper is a little long, center it and let the ends extend beyond the bands. Center the zipper in the bag opening and sew the bands to the front and back panels. Tuck any extra length inside the bag. Tack the ends to the gusset strip if necessary.

Shoulder Strap

Cut nylon webbing and singe ends to prevent raveling. Insert webbing into one end of the gusset tube, working in and out of the slits as you come to them. Slide one buckle onto each end of strap. Slide on the shoulder pad. Fasten the two ends of the shoulder strap with the buckles. Trim strap to suit your needs, leaving room for adjustment.

Pull ends of gusset strip up the strap to remove slack. Sew a few large sts through both sides of gusset panel and strap to stabilize bag and strap.

If you don't like sewing by hand, assemble this bag with a heavy-duty sewing machine.

To give this triangular purse plenty of depth, Norah Gaughan sewed gussets at the base as well as generous pleats on the front and back. She double-crocheted the wide lower section in a suede-look nylon yarn and single-crocheted the upper part in a fuzzy wool/alpaca blend that she later felted. To make it easy to find things in the purse, Norah sewed the side seams along the lower section only—the upper part stretches open. A cardboard insert lends stability to the base, and a fabric lining helps the un-felted section hold its shape. There's no need for a fastener; the smart leather handles hold the bag closed as it's carried.

BODY

With MC, ch 65. Dc into 4th chain from hook and in each ch across, turn—63 dc. Ch 3, dc into next st and in each st across, turn. Work even in dc until piece measures 18" (45.5 cm) from beg. Fasten off.

Pleat

Mark the center of chain edge and last row. Mark 2" (5 cm) out from center marker (point A), then mark 2" (5 cm) out from these markers (point B) as shown. Bring point B to center point, folding along lines A and B on both sides of center point. With yarn threaded on a tapestry needle, baste in place.

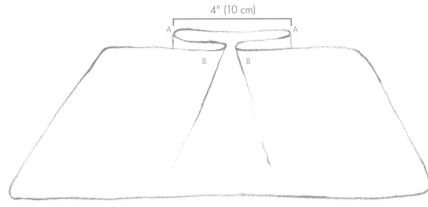

Fold the upper edge into a wide pleat.

FINISHED SIZE

About 13" (33 cm) wide at base, 11½" (29 cm) tall, and 3" (7.5 cm) deep.

YARN

Worsted weight (#4 Medium).

Shown here: Berroco Suede (100% nylon; 120 yd [110 m]/50 g): #3734 mattunuck (MC), 3 balls. Berroco Ultra Alpaca (50% alpaca, 50% wool; 215 yd [197 m]/100 g): #6277 peat mix (CC), 1 skein.

HOOK

Size G/6 (4 mm). Adjust hook size if necessary to obtain the correct gauge.

NOTIONS

Removable markers; tapestry needle; net laundry bag; 1 pair 12" (30.5 cm) leather handles; ¼ yd (0.25 m) lining fabric; 3" x 13" (7.5 x 33 cm) piece of cardboard for stiffening bottom.

GAUGE

14 double crochet = 4" (10 cm) with suede.

Smooth leather handles
impart a dressy look.

Top

With CC and RS facing, work 40 sc across one pleated side, working through all layers of pleat. Work even in sc for 11 more rows. Sc2tog at beg of every row 10 times—30 sc rem. Fasten off. Rep for other side.

FINISHING

Weave in loose ends.

Felting

Place bag in net laundry bag and run through washer cycle set on small load, hot wash, and cold rinse, adding a small amount of mild detergent. Stop the washer periodically to check the progress of the felting; run through additional cycles if necessary until bottom of felted portion measures about 8" (20.5 cm) across and felted portion is firm.

Gussets

With MC threaded on a tapestry needle, sew side seams. Turn bag inside out and hold upside down. Flatten out the bottom of the bag so that the fold line is centered, forming a point at each side (see Design Notebook, pages 106–107). With tapestry needle, sew base 2½" (6.5 cm) in from each side. Fold points up toward sides of bag and sew tips of points to side seams.

Lining

Cut a 7" x 14" (18 x 35.5 cm) piece of lining fabric. Fold fabric lengthwise with RS tog and, using a ½" (1.3 cm) seam allowance, sew long sides tog. Sew one short side. Turn RS out, insert cardboard into lining pouch and slip st end of pouch closed. Insert fabric-covered cardboard into bottom of bag so that it lies flat. Cut a 36" x 10" (91.5 x 25.5 cm) piece of lining fabric. With sewing needle, matching thread, and RS tog, sew short sides tog. Sew bottom seam and miter corners as for bag. Fold down top edge ½" (1.3 cm) to WS. Make pleats in lining as for bag. With WS tog, sew lining into bag.

With CC threaded on a tapestry needle, sew bag handles to felted portion of bag.

Give your bag more depth by adding a couple of carefully placed pleats.

HEMP MARKET BAG
KATIE HIMMELBERG

A champion of string market bags, **Katie Himmelberg** designed this one to be wider than most so that it could hold long veggies, leafy greens, fresh baguettes, and other goodies with ease. She worked the body of the bag in a single piece from the edging at the top of one side down to the base and up again to the edging on the other side. Then she seamed along the sides. She chose a stretch lace pattern to give the bag plenty of flexibility and worked it in a strong hemp yarn for durability. Stitches for the strap are picked up along the top of the bag at one side seam, then worked in garter stitch for the desired length and sewn to the top edge at the opposite side.

STITCH GUIDE

Point d'Esprit (multiple of 6 sts + 9)

Row 1: (RS) K2 *yo, k2tog, k1, k2tog, yo, k1; rep from * to last 7 sts, yo, k2tog, k1, k2tog, yo, k2.

Row 2: K3, *yo, sl 1, k2tog, psso, yo, k3; rep from *.

Row 3: K2, k2tog, *yo, k1, yo, k2tog, k1, k2tog; rep from * to last 5 sts, yo, k1, yo, k2tog, k2.

Row 4: K1, k2tog, *yo, k3, yo, sl 1, k2tog, psso; rep from * to last 6 sts, yo, k3, yo, k2tog, k1.

Repeat Rows 1–4 for pattern.

BAG

With size 7 needles, CO 65 sts.

Edging

Work in garter st (knit every row) for 4 rows. Change to size 8 needles and knit 4 more rows. Change to size 9 needles and knit 4 more rows. *Next row:* Change to size 10 needles and use the M1 method (see Glossary, page 123) to inc 4 sts evenly spaced—69 sts. Knit 3 more rows.

FINISHED SIZE

About 26¼" (66.5 cm) wide at base, 14½" (37 cm) wide at top, and 13¼" (33.5 cm) tall.

YARN

DK weight (#3 Light).

Shown here: Lanaknits Hemp for Knitting allhemp6 (100% hemp; 165 yd [151 m]/100 g): sprout (yellow-green), 2 skeins.

NEEDLES

Body—size 13 (9 mm). Edging—sizes 7, 8, 9, and 10 (4.5, 5, 5.5, and 6 mm). Adjust needle size if necessary to obtain the correct gauge.

NOTIONS

Tapestry needle.

GAUGE

10½ stitches and 14 rows = 4" (10 cm) in stitch pattern on largest needles; 18 stitches and 36 rows = 4" (10 cm) in garter stitch on smallest needles.

Body

Change to size 13 needles. Work Rows 1–4 of point d'esprit patt (see Stitch Guide) 20 times—piece measures about 24½" (62 cm) from CO.

Edging

Change to size 10 needles and knit 3 rows. *Next row:* knit, dec 4 sts (k2tog) evenly spaced—65 sts rem. Change to size 9 needles and knit 4 rows. Change to size 8 needles and knit 4 rows. Change to size 7 needles and knit 4 rows. Loosely BO all sts.

FINISHING

Fold bag in half with RS tog, meeting CO edge to BO edge. With yarn threaded on a tapestry needle, use a whipstitch (see Glossary, page 124) to sew side seams.

Strap

With smallest needles and RS facing, pick up and knit 10 sts centered above one side seam. Work in garter st until piece measures 18" (45.5 cm). BO all sts. Center end of strap over other side seam and whipstitch in place.

Weave in loose ends. Steam-press lightly to open up lace patt.

Paper or plastic? Neither—go green with a handknitted bag!

This lacy stitch pattern stretches in width and length to accommodate a variety of groceries.

LINEN TUBE CLUTCH
RUTHIE NUSSBAUM

On a recent trip to the Bahamas, Ruthie Nussbaum was fascinated by the intricately woven straw baskets, bags, and placemats in the Straw Market of downtown Nassau. She translated these shapes, textures, and colors into this unusual linen clutch. Ruthie knitted the bag in two layers—a stockinette-stitch inner layer and a textured outer layer—and sandwiched flexible plastic needlepoint canvas between the two. She sewed the layers to knitted circles to give the bag its distinctive shape, then finished it with a few rows of crochet with built-in handles.

STITCH GUIDE

Herringbone Stitch

Row 1: (RS) *K2tog through back loop (tbl), slip first st off left-hand needle and leave second st on needle; rep from * to last st, k1tbl.

Row 2: *P2tog, slip first st off needle and leave second st on needle; rep from * to last st, p1.

Repeat Rows 1 and 2 for pattern.

OUTER BAG

With larger needles and 2 strands of yarn held tog, CO 80 sts. Rep Rows 1 and 2 of herringbone st (see Stitch Guide) until piece measures 10¾" (27.5 cm) from CO, ending with a WS row. With RS facing, BO all sts in patt.

INNER BAG

With smaller needles and single strand of yarn, CO 54 sts. Work even in St st until piece measures 13½" (34.5 cm) from CO. BO all sts.

FINISHED SIZE

About 10¾" (27.5 cm) wide, 5" (12.5 cm) tall, and 5" (12.5 cm) deep, excluding handles.

YARN

Sportweight (#2 Fine).

Shown here: Louet Euroflax Sport Weight (100% wet-spun linen; 270 yd [247 m]/ 100 g): #35 mustard, 3 skeins.

NEEDLES

Outer bag—size 9 (5.5 mm): straight and set of 4 double-pointed (dpn). Inner bag—size 4 (3.5 mm). Adjust needle size if necessary to obtain the correct gauge.

NOTIONS

Marker (m); tapestry needle; size F/5 (3.75 mm) crochet hook; 1 sheet 10½" (26.5 cm) by 13½" (34.5 cm) and two 5" (12.5 cm) circles of plastic needlepoint canvas.

GAUGE

20 stitches and 30 rows = 4" (10 cm) in stockinette stitch with single strand on smaller needles; 16 stitches and 22 rows = 4" (10 cm) in stockinette stitch with yarn doubled on larger needles; 23 stitches and 18 rows = 4" (10 cm) in herringbone pattern with yarn doubled on larger needles.

END CIRCLE (MAKE 2)

With dpn and 2 strands of yarn held tog, CO 6 sts. Arrange sts evenly on 3 dpn, place marker (pm), and join for working in the rnd, being careful not to twist sts.

Rnd 1 and all odd-numbered rnds: Knit.

Rnd 2: K1f&b (see Glossary, page 124) in every st—12 sts.

Rnd 4: *K1, k1f&b; rep from *—18 sts.

Rnd 6: *K2, k1f&b; rep from *—24 sts.

Rnd 8: *K3, k1f&b; rep from *—30 sts.

Rnd 10: *K4, k1f&b; rep from *—36 sts.

Rnd 12: *K5, k1f&b; rep from *—42 sts.

Rnd 14: *K6, k1f&b; rep from *—48 sts.

Loosely BO all sts.

FINISHING

Block pieces. Weave in loose ends.

Assembly

Layer outer bag, needlepoint canvas, and inner bag, with RS of each knitted piece facing out as shown at below. With yarn threaded on a tapestry needle, baste edges. With 2 strands of yarn held tog and RS facing, beg at corner of bag layers, use single crochet (sc; see Glossary, page 122, for crochet instructions) to join one end circle to the long edge of the bag layers, working one sc in each BO st of the circle and working through all layers—there will be about 5 sts of the circle left unworked when you reach the corner, ch 1 at corner, work 36 sc evenly spaced along top edge of bag, ch 1 at corner, then attach second end circle as before, ch 1 at fourth corner, and work 36 sc evenly spaced across other top edge. Do not cut yarn.

Plastic needlepoint canvas will hold any shape.

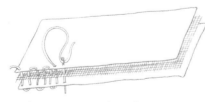

Baste bag pieces around needlepoint canvas.

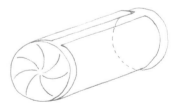

Join end cirlces to layered bag peices.

Handles

Row 1: Turn, ch 1, sc in each sc across top edge of bag, turn.

Row 2: Ch 1, sc in each sc across, turn.

Row 3: Ch 1, sc in first 12 sc, ch 12, skip 12 sc, sc in last 12 sc, turn.

Rows 4–7: Ch 1, sc in each st across, turn.

Row 8: Ch 1, sc in first 12 sc, ch 12, skip 12 sc, sc in last 12 sc, turn.

Row 9: Ch 1, sc in each st across, turn.

Row 10: Ch 1, sc in each sc across.

Fasten off. Weave in loose ends.

Fold handle in half and with yarn threaded on a tapestry needle, use a whipstitch (see Glossary, page 126) to sew Row 10 edge to WS of bag. Whipstitch around handle slit. Whipstitch selvedge edges of handle closed. Join yarn to other side of bag and rep for other handle.

Place a circle of needlepoint canvas behind each end circle on inside of bag.

The handles on this bag are worked into the crochet edging along the opening.

With an unusual twist on knitting yarn, **Bri Ana Drennon** and **Regina Rioux Gonzalez** designed this generous tote to be crocheted in raffia ribbon. A stiff oval base is worked in rounds of single crochet with a double strand of raffia. The flexible body of the bag is then worked upward from the base with a single strand of raffia and finished with graceful scallops. Sturdy crocheted straps worked in the contrast color run from the base to the top of the bag, and a row of single-crochet piping edges the top and calls out the sides of the gussets. For a final touch, an apple-motif pocket is attached to the front. No additional fastener or lining is needed.

BASE

With 2 strands of MC held tog and larger hook, ch 25.

Rnd 1: Sc in 2nd ch from hook and in next 22 ch, 4 sc in last ch, rotate and sc in each of next 23 ch along the bottom of foundation ch, 4 sc in last ch, join with sl st in beg sc—54 sts total.

Rnd 2: Ch 1, sc in first 23 sc, [2 sc in next sc] 4 times, sc in next 23 sc, [2 sc in next sc] 4 times, join with sl st in beg sc—62 sts.

Rnd 3: Ch 1, sc in first 24 sc, 2 sc in next sc, sc in next sc, [2 sc in next sc] 2 times, sc in next sc, 2 sc in next sc, sc in next 25 sc, 2 sc in next sc, sc in next sc, [2 sc in next sc] 2 times, sc in next sc, 2 sc in next sc, sc in next sc, join with sl st in beg sc—70 sts.

Rnd 4: Ch 1, sc in first 25 sc, 2 sc in next sc, sc in next 2 sc, [2 sc in next sc] 2 times, sc in next 2 sc, 2 sc in next sc, sc in next 27 sc, 2 sc in next sc, sc in next 2 sc, [2 sc in next sc] 2 times, sc in next 2 sc, 2 sc in next sc, sc in next 2 sc, join with sl st in beg sc—78 sts.

Rnd 5: Ch 1, sc in first 26 sc, 2 sc in next sc, sc in next 3 sc, [2 sc in next sc] 2 times, sc in next 3 sc, 2 sc in next sc, sc in next 29 sc, 2 sc in next sc, sc in next 3 sc, [2 sc in next sc] 2 times, sc in next 3 sc, 2 sc in next sc, sc in next 3 sc, join with sl st in beg sc—86 sts.

Rnd 6: Ch 1, sc in first 27 sc, 2 sc in next sc, sc in next 4 sc, [2 sc in next sc] 2 times, sc in next 4 sc, 2 sc in next sc, sc in next 31 sc, 2 sc in next sc, sc in next 4 sc, [2 sc in next sc] 2 times, sc in next 4 sc, 2 sc in next sc, sc in next 4 sc, join with sl st in beg sc—94 sts.

FINISHED SIZE

16½" (42 cm) wide and 7½" (19 cm) deep at base, 53½" (136 cm) circumference at top, and 11¼" (28.5 cm) tall, excluding straps.

YARN

Shown here: ¼" (6 mm) Wraffia Ribbon (100% raffia; 100 yd [91 m]/spool): #4434810 white (MC), 8 spools; #4434830 red (CC), 2 spools; #4434865 kelly green, and #4434820 black, less than 1 spool each.

HOOK

Bag—size I/9 (5.5 mm). Pocket—size G/6 (4 mm). Adjust hook size if necessary to obtain the correct gauge.

NOTIONS

Removable markers; tapestry needle.

GAUGE

12 single crochet and 13 rounds = 4" (10 cm) with double strand of ribbon on larger hook; 13 single crochet and 15 rounds = 4" (10 cm) with single strand of ribbon on larger hook; 16 single crochet and 16 rows = 4" (10 cm) with single strand of ribbon on smaller hook.

Raffia ribbon is a natural alternative to yarn.

Rnd 7: Ch 1, sc in first 28 sc, 2 sc in next sc, sc in next 5 sc, [2 sc in next sc] 2 times, sc in next 5 sc, 2 sc in next sc, sc in next 33 sc, 2 sc in next sc, sc in next 5 sc, [2 sc in next sc] 2 times, sc in next 5 sc, 2 sc in next sc, sc in next 5 sc, join with sl st in beg sc—102 sts.

Rnd 8: Ch 1, sc in first 29 sc, 2 sc in next sc, sc in next 6 sc, [2sc in next sc] 2 times, sc in next 6 sc, 2 sc in next sc, sc in next 35 sc, 2 sc in next sc, sc in next 6 sc, [2 st in next sc] 2 times, sc in next 6 sc, 2 sc in next sc, sc in next 6 sc, join with sl st in beg sc—110 sts.

Rnds 9–12: Ch 1, sc in each sc around, join with sl st in beg sc.

BODY

Fasten off 1 strand of ribbon and cont working body with 1 strand only.

Rnd 13: Ch 1, working in back loops for entire rnd, sc in first 28 sc, 2 sc in next sc, sc in next 9 sc, [2 sc in next sc] 2 times, sc in next 9 sc, 2 sc in next sc, sc in next 33 sc, 2 sc in next sc, sc in next 9 sc, [2 sc in next sc] 2 times, sc in next 9 sc, 2 sc in next sc, sc in next 5 sc, join with sl st in beg sc—118 sts.

Rnd 14: Ch 1, sc in each sc around, join with sl st in beg sc.

Rnd 15: Ch 1, sc in first 28 sc, 2 sc in next sc, sc in next 11 sc, [2 sc in next sc] 2 times, sc in next 11 sc, 2 sc in next sc, sc in next 33 sc, 2 sc in next sc, sc in next 11 sc, [2 sc in next sc] 2 times, sc in next 11 sc, 2 sc in next sc, sc in next 5 sc, join with sl st in beg sc—126 sts.

Rnds 16 and 17: Ch 1, sc in each sc around, join with sl st in beg sc.

Rnd 18: Ch 1, sc in first 28 sc, 2 sc in next sc, sc in next 13 sc, [2 sc in next sc] 2 times, sc in next 13 sc, 2 sc in next sc, sc in next 33 sc, 2 sc in next sc, sc in next 13 sc, [2 sc in next sc] 2 times, sc in next 13 sc, 2 sc in next sc, sc in next 5 sc, join with sl st in beg sc—134 sts.

Rnds 19–21: Ch 1, sc in each sc around, join with sl st in beg sc.

Rnd 22: Ch 1, sc in first 28 sc, 2 sc in next sc, sc in next 15 sc, [2 sc in next sc] 2 times, sc in next 15 sc, 2 sc in next sc, sc in next 33 sc, 2 sc in next sc, sc in next 15 sc, [2 sc in next sc] 2 times, sc in next 15 sc, 2 sc in next sc, sc in next 5 sc, join with sl st in beg sc—142 sts.

Rnds 23–26: Ch 1, sc in each sc around, join with sl st in beg sc.

Rnd 27: Ch 1, sc in first 28 sc, 2 sc in next sc, sc in next 17 sc, [2 sc in next sc] 2 times, sc in next 17 sc, 2 sc in next sc, sc in next 33 sc, 2 sc in next sc, sc in next 17 sc, [2 sc in next sc] 2 times, sc in next 17 sc, 2 sc in next sc, sc in next 5 sc, join with sl st in beg sc—150 sts.

Rnds 28–31: Ch 1, sc in each sc around, join with sl st in beg sc.

Rnd 32: Ch 1, sc in first 28 sc, 2 sc in next sc, sc in next 19 sc, [2 sc in next sc] 2 times, sc in next 19 sc, 2 sc in next sc, sc in next 33 sc, 2 sc in next sc, sc in next 19 sc, [2 sc in next sc] 2 times, sc in next 19 sc, 2 sc in next sc, sc in next 5 sc, join with sl st in beg sc—158 sts.

Rnds 33–37: Ch 1, sc in each sc around, join with sl st in beg sc.

Rnd 38: Ch 1, sc in first 28 sc, 2 sc in next sc, sc in next 21 sc, [2 sc in next sc] 2 times, sc in next 21 sc, 2 sc in next sc, sc in next 33 sc, 2 sc in next sc, sc in next 21 sc, [2 sc in next sc] 2 times, sc in next 21 sc, 2 sc in next sc, sc in next 5 sc, join with sl st to beg sc—166 sts.

Rnds 39–43: Ch 1, sc in each sc around, join with sl st in beg sc.

Rnd 44: Ch 1, sc in first 28 sc, 2 sc in next sc, sc in next 23 sc, [2 sc in next sc] 2 times, sc in next 23 sc, 2 sc in next sc, sc in next 33 sc, 2 sc in next sc, sc in next 23 sc, [2 sc in next sc] 2 times, sc in next 23 sc, 2 sc in next sc, sc in next 5 sc, join with sl st to beg sc—174 sts.

Rnds 45–54: Ch 1, sc in each sc around, join with sl st in beg sc. Do not fasten off.

Back Scallop

Cont in rows as foll:

Row 1: Ch 1, sc in first 26 sc, turn.

Row 2: Ch 1, sc in first 29 sc, turn.

Row 3: Ch 1, sc in first 27 sc, turn.

Row 4: Ch 1, sc in first 25 sc, turn.

Row 5: Ch 1, sc in first 22 sc, turn.

Row 6: Ch 1, sc in first 19 sc, turn.

Row 7: Ch 1, sc in first 15 sc. Fasten off.

Right Side Scallop

With RS facing, join MC to 5th st to left of back scallop (4 open sts between back scallop and right side scallop).

Row 1: Ch 1, sc in first 16 sc, turn.

Row 2: Ch 1, sc2tog, sc in next sc, sc2tog, turn.

Row 3: Ch 1, sc2tog, sc in next 10 sc, sc2tog, turn.

Row 4: Ch 1, sc2tog, sc in next 8 sc, sc2tog, turn.

Row 5: Ch 1, sc2tog, sc in next 6 sc, sc2tog, turn.

Row 6: Ch 1, sc2tog, sc in next 4 sc, sc2tog. Fasten off.

Middle Side Scallop

With RS facing, join MC to 2nd st to left of right side scallop (1 open st between right side scallop and middle side scallop). Work Rows 1–6 as for right side scallop.

Raffia is as flexible as yarn, especially strong, and comes in some great colors.

Left Side Scallop

With RS facing, join MC to 2nd st to left of middle side scallop (1 open st between middle side scallop and left side scallop). Work Rows 1–6 as for right side scallop.

Front Scallop

With RS facing, join MC to 5th st to left of left side scallop (4 open sts between left side scallop and front scallop). Work Rows 2–7 of back scallop.

Right Side Scallop

With RS facing, join MC to 5th st to left of front scallop (4 open sts between front scallop and right side scallop). Work Rows 1–6 as for previous right side scallop.

Middle Side Scallop

With RS facing, join MC to 2nd st to left of right side scallop (1 open st between right side scallop and middle side scallop). Work Rows 1–6 as for right side scallop.

Left Side Scallop

With RS facing, join MC to 2nd st to left of middle side scallop (1 open st between middle side scallop and left side scallop). Work Rows 1–6 as for right side scallop, but do not fasten off after Row 6—4 open sts rem between left side scallop and back scallop.

Top Border

This rnd finishes off the scallops and changes the stair-step edges to smooth semicircles. Crochet along the flat surface of the steps on the front and back scallops (not into the sides of those rows) and crochet into the sides of the rows on the side scallops. Work as foll: With MC still attached and RS facing, ch 1, work 6 sc along top of scallop, 8 sc evenly spaced down side of scallop, 4 sc in between scallops, working up large scallop skip side of row and work 2 sc in row above, skip side and work 3 sc in row above, skip side and work 15 sc across top of scallop, working down scallop skip side and work 4 sc in row below, skip side and work 3 sc into row below, skip side and work 2 sc in row below, skip side and work 4 sc into row below in between scallops, [8 sc evenly spaced up side of scallop, 6 sc across top of scallop, 8 sc evenly spaced down side of scallop, 1 sc in between scallops] 3 times, 3 more sc in between scallops, working up large scallop skip side of row and work 2 sc in row above, skip side of row and work 3 sc in row above, skip side of row and work 4 sc in row above, skip side of row and work 15 sc along top of scallop, skip side of row and work 3 sc in row below, skip side of row and work 2 sc in row below, skip side of row and work 4 sc in row below in between scallops, [8 sc evenly spaced up side of scallop, 6 sc across top of scallop, 8 sc evenly spaced down side of scallop, 1 sc in between scallops] 2 times, 8 sc evenly spaced up side of scallop, join with sl st in beg sc. Fasten off.

Carefully placed increases cause the bag to taper gently from the base to the top.

PIPING

All piping is worked with a single strand of CC and larger hook.

Side Piping

To begin, locate one of the single sc sts in the previously completed border rnd that can be found on either side of a middle side scallop (1 st before and 1 st after the curved edge of each middle side scallop—4 individual sts total around top of bag). Insert hook from right to left into the post of 1 of the 4 indicated sts and work a sc, cont by working into the st directly below the st just made, inserting hook from right to left into the post to make 1 post sc. Cont in this fashion, working each st directly below the one just completed to the base of the bag—44 sts total. Fasten off. Rep for 3 other sides.

Bottom Piping

Loosely work 1 sc into the front loop of each sc of Rnd 12, join with sl st in beg sc. Fasten off.

Top Piping

Work 1 rnd of sc along top of bag, join with sl st in beg sc. Fasten off.

The apple detail is really a small pocket for change or keys.

STRAPS (MAKE 2)

With a single strand of CC and larger hook, ch 171.

Row 1: Sc in 2nd ch from hook and in each ch across, turn—170 sts.

Rows 2–4: Ch 1, sc in each sc across, turn.

Fasten off.

POCKET

With a single strand of MC and smaller hook, ch 6.

Row 1: Sc in 2nd ch from hook and in each ch across, turn—5 sc.

Row 2: Ch 3, sc in 2nd ch from hook and in each ch across, turn—7 sc.

Row 3: Ch 3, sc in 2nd ch from hook and in next 7 sc, 2 sc in last sc, turn—10 sts.

Row 4: Ch 1, 2 sc in first sc, sc in next 8 sc, 2 sc in last sc, turn—12 sts.

Row 5: Ch 1, sc in first 11 sc, 2 sc in last sc, turn—13 sts.

Row 6: Ch 1, 2 sc in first sc, sc in next 12 sc, turn—14 sts.

Row 7: Ch 1, sc in first 13 sc, 2 sc in last sc, turn—15 sts.

Row 8: Ch 1, sc in first 13 sc, sc2tog, turn—14 sts rem.

Row 9: Ch 1, sc2tog, sc in next 12 sc, turn—13 sts rem.

Row 10: Ch 1, sc in each sc across, turn.

Cut off MC and join CC. Cont as foll:

Row 11: Ch 1, sc in each sc across, turn.

Row 12: Ch 1, sc in first 12 sc, 2 sc in last sc, turn—14 sts.

Row 13: Ch 1, 2 sc in first sc, sc in next 13 sc, turn—15 sts.

Row 14: Ch 1, sc2tog, sc in next 13 sc, turn—14 sts rem.

Row 15: Ch 1, sc in first 12 sc, sc2tog, turn—13 sts rem.

Row 16: Ch 1, sc2tog, sc in next 11 sc, turn—12 sts rem.

Row 17: Ch 1, sc2tog, sc in next 8 sc, sc2tog, turn—10 sts rem.

Row 18: Ch 1, sc2tog, sc in next 8 sc, turn—9 sts rem.

Row 19: Ch 1, [sc2tog] 2 times, sc in next sc, [sc2tog] 2 times—5 sts rem. Do not turn; do not fasten off.

Inside Border

Place marker on last st completed. Beg and end at marker, work 2 rnds sc around entire pocket. Fasten off. This is the RS of motif.

Leaf

With RS facing and smaller hook, join green to apple just right of ctenter above white portion of motif.

Row 1: Ch 1, sc in first 6 sc, turn.

Row 2: Ch 1, sc2tog, sc in next 3 sc, 2 sc in last sc, turn—6 sts.

Row 3: Ch 1, sc in first 2 sc, [sc2tog] 2 times, turn—4 sts rem.

Row 4: Ch 1, sc2tog, sc in next sc, 2 sc in last sc, turn—4 sts.

Row 5: Ch 1, sc in first 2 sc. Fasten off.

Outside Border

With MC and smaller hook, work 1 rnd of sc around entire pocket (including leaf), working 2 sc in 1 st around apex of curved portion to prevent puckers. Fasten off.

FINISHING

Weave in loose ends.

Straps

Position strap between front scallop and side scallop. With CC and beg at lower edge of bag, sew strap to bag. Sew other end of strap to other side of front scallop in the same manner, being careful not to twist strap. Repeat for back of bag.

Join Pocket

With black, embroider four "seeds" onto front of pocket. With MC, sew pocket to bag front.

FELT LAPTOP CASE
KATE JACKSON

For a fresh alternative to the black nylon laptop bag, Kate Jackson knitted and felted her own jazzy striped version. She worked the body of this bag in one piece from side to side, beginning and ending with extra strips to make pleats that provide necessary depth. Then she knitted a separate piece for the shoulder strap, which she made long enough to extend all the way to the base of the bag. For stability and strength, Kate felted the whole thing, then she added a little embroidery detail to make it clearly her own.

> **NOTE**
> ✤ Take time to check your gauge. Because the bag will be felted, exact gauge is not crucial for the finished size of the bag, but you'll want to be sure not to run out of yarn.

PLEAT (MAKE 2)
With CC, CO 70 sts. Beg with a RS row, work in St st for 28 rows. Place sts on holder. Make another piece to match.

BODY
With MC and RS facing, knit across the 70 sts of one pleat piece, then use the backward-loop method (see Glossary, page 121) to CO 18 sts, then knit across the 70 sts of the other pleat piece as shown on page 54 —158 sts total. Knit the next (WS) row. Cont in St st for 159 rows as foll: 28 rows MC, 24 rows CC, 14 rows MC, 16 rows CC, 18 rows MC, 8 rows CC, 51 rows MC, ending with a RS row. Knit 1 (WS) row. *Next row:* K70, BO 18 sts, knit to end—70 sts rem each side. Working each side separately, join CC and work in St st for 28 rows for two pleats on other side. BO all sts.

STRAP AND BAG SIDES
With MC, CO 18 sts. Work in St st for 94 rows. Place removable marker on the last row. Cont as foll: *RS rows:* Knit. *WS rows:* K1, p16, k1. Rep these 2 rows until a total of 230 rows have been worked after marker. Place removable marker on the last row. Cont even in St st for 94 rows. BO all sts.

FINISHED SIZE
18" (45.5 cm) wide, 12½" (31.5 cm) tall and 9½" (24 cm) deep after felting.

YARN
Worsted weight (#4 Medium).
Shown here: Cascade Yarns Cascade 220 (100% wool; 220 yd [201 m]/100 g): #9420 dark teal (MC), 4 skeins; #8914 lime (CC), 3 skeins.

NEEDLES
Size 10½ (6.5 mm). Adjust needle size if necessary to obtain the correct gauge.

NOTIONS
Removable markers; stitch holders; tapestry needle; pillowcase; felting needle (optional).

GAUGE
14 stitches and 18 rows = 4" (10 cm) in stockinette stitch before felting.

You may be a computer geek, but you don't have to look like one!

Knit across one pleat, cast on 18 stitches, then knit across the other pleat.

```
        pleat                    pleat


                      body


        pleat                    pleat
```

End the body by working the pleat stitiches separately to match the pleats at the cast-on edge.

FINISHING

With MC threaded on a tapestry needle, sew CO and BO edges of strap to the gaps between the pleats on the bag body, being careful not to twist strap. Sew CO and BO edges of pleats to the side of the strap, matching the marked rows to the tops of the pleats. Fold the pleats into box pleats as shown below and stitch them along the top and bottom edges to secure. Weave in loose ends.

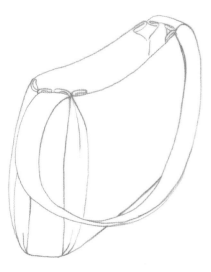

Fold the pleats to the inside of the bag and secure along the top and bottom edges.

The pleats are worked in a contrasting yarn for an unsuspected kick of color.

Felting

Place bag into a pillowcase and close with a rubber band. Put it in the washing machine with a pair of old jeans and a small amount of regular detergent. Set the washer to a small load, regular agitation, hot wash, and cold rinse cycle. Allow washer to go through the cycle, stopping and checking during the agitation periods, and repeating the agitation if necessary until the stitches disappear and the bag shrinks to desired size. It is a good idea to stretch the fabric every time you check it to encourage even felting. When the bag has reached its finished size, let it go through the spin cycle to remove excess water. Lay it on a flat surface, stretch it into shape, and let air-dry.

Trim off any yarn ends close to the fabric. With a steam iron, press the pleats into shape and smooth out any wrinkles left from felting.

Monogram (optional)

Position a strand of CC to outline a monogram or symbol as desired on bag front. Use a felting needle to stab the yarn into place. Repeat with another strand of yarn for a bolder monogram.

FAIR ISLE BOOK BAG
KRISTIN NICHOLAS

The rectangular book bag is the bread and butter of knitted bags. In this version, Kristin Nicholas began with a flat base, then picked up stitches around the edges and worked the body in the round to the upper edge, alternating a few rounds of stockinette stitch and reverse stockinette stitch to punctuate the base and top. For the handles, she braided two lengths of the main color, felted them for strength, and sewed them securely in place. Then she added bright embroidery to one side of the bag (feel free to add it to both sides or to leave it out altogether), and she finished the bag by inserting a piece of plastic needlepoint canvas in the base and lining it with a woven fabric.

BAG
With A, CO 46 sts.

Base
Work back and forth in garter st (knit every row) for 16 rows—8 garter ridges.

Sides
With A and RS facing, pick up and knit sts along rem 3 sides of base as foll: 9 sts along short side, 46 sts along CO edge, 9 sts along other short side—110 sts total. Place marker (pm) and join for working in the rnd. Purl 2 rnds. Change to B and knit 1 rnd, then purl 2 rnds. Change to A and knit 1 rnd, then purl 1 rnd. *Inc rnd:* *P11, use the backward-loop method (see Glossary, page 119) to CO 1 st; rep from * 9 more times—120 sts. Rep Rnds 1–12 of Fair Isle chart until piece measures 13" (33 cm) from beg of charted patt. *Dec rnd:* With A, *k10, k2tog; rep from *—110 sts rem. With A, purl 2 rnds. Change to B and knit 1 rnd, then purl 2 rnds. Change to A and knit 1 rnd, then purl 2 rnds. With B, BO all sts kwise.

FINISHED SIZE
17½" (44.5 cm) wide at base, 13¾" (35 cm) wide at center of bag, 16½" (42 cm) tall and 3½" (9 cm) deep.

YARN
Chunky weight (#5 Bulky).

Shown here: Nashua Handknits Creative Focus Chunky (75% wool, 25% alpaca; 110 yd [101 m]/100 g]: #CFC2124 cordovan (reddish-brown; A), 4 balls; #CFC1117 grass (green; B), 3 balls; #CFC1590 brilliant blue (C), 1 ball.

NEEDLES
Size 9 (5.5 mm): 24" (60 cm) circular (cir). Adjust needle size if necessary to obtain the correct gauge.

NOTIONS
Marker (m); tapestry needle; ½ yd (0.5 meter) tightly woven cotton fabric for lining; sewing machine (optional); sharp-point sewing needle; matching thread; straight pins; 3½" x 17½" (9 x 44.5 cm) piece of plastic needlepoint canvas.

GAUGE
14 stitches and 16 rounds = 4" (10 cm) in Fair Isle pattern.

The essential book bag—a classic among classics.

Fair Isle

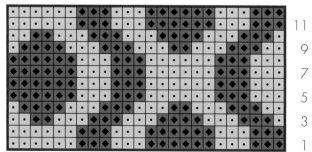

11
9
7
5
3
1

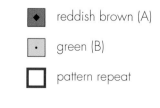

FINISHING

Weave in loose ends.

Embroidery

With C threaded on a tapestry needle, work a 4-pointed daisy st (see Glossary, page 121) in the center of each oval shape on front of bag. Using a running st (see Glossary, page 122), work dotted lines through the center of each undulating line on front of bag.

Handles (make 2)

Cut 24 lengths of A, each 72" (183 cm) long. Tie one end into an overhand knot. Divide the strands into 3 groups of 8 strands each and work a 3-strand braid for the length of the strands. Tie the ends into an overhand knot. Felt in the washing machine. With a sewing needle and matching thread, sew knotted ends of handles securely to right side of bag, flattening out knots as you do so, as shown below.

Lining

Note: Instructions here are for using a sewing machine; you may sew the lining by hand as well. Cut a piece of lining fabric 1" (2.5 cm) wider than the bag width and twice the bag height plus 1" (2.5 cm). Fold the fabric in half widthwise with RS tog. Using a sewing machine, sew each side with a ½" (1.3 cm) seam allowance. Fold the top open edge down ½" (1.3 cm) to WS and press. Insert plastic needlepoint canvas into bottom of bag. Insert lining into bag with WS tog. With a sewing needle and matching thread, sew folded top edge of lining to top edge of bag.

Add simple embroidery to brighten up the two-color Fair Isle pattern.

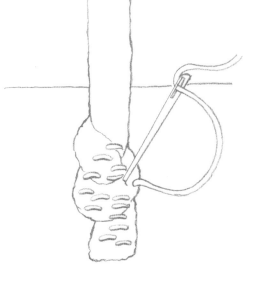

Sew knotted ends of handles securely to right side of bag.

In an unusual twist on bag construction, **Lisa Daehlin** began with two circular doily motifs worked from the center outward to a decorative picot edge. She picked up stitches around the perimeter of the doily circles and worked a wide gusset to give the bag depth, leaving an opening at the center top for a two-way zipper closure (trimmed with I-cord). Circles cut from plastic needlepoint canvas and stitched inside a woven fabric liner help the purse keep its shape and show off the lace pattern. The short handle is knitted in a double thickness, edged with picots, then knitted right into the join where the bag front and back meet the gusset.

HANDLE

With cir needle and using the invisible method (see Glossary, page 120), provisionally CO 39 sts. Do not join into a rnd. Beg with a WS (knit) row, work 10 rows in rev St st (purl RS rows; knit WS rows), ending with a purl row. Work picot-trimmed edge as foll: Purl 1 row, knit 1 row, purl 1 row. *Picot row:* K1, *yo, k2tog; rep from * to end of row. Purl 1 row, knit 1 row, purl 1 row. Place each purl bump from WS of first row of St st 7 rows below onto smaller dpn, fold work along picot row so that purl sides of picot edge face tog and so that smaller dpn is parallel to and behind working dpn. Knit 1 row, working the sts from the two needles tog as if to k2tog—still 39 sts. Beg with a knit row, cont in rev St st for 20 more rows, ending with a purl row. Work another picot-trimmed edge as before (8 rows total). Beg with a knit row, cont in rev St st for 10 more rows. Remove waste yarn from provisional CO and place 39 exposed loops on a spare dpn. Fold work in half so that picot edgings face tog and so that the needle with the CO sts is parallel to and behind the needle with the live sts. Use the three-needle BO (see Glossary, page 119) to join live sts to exposed CO loops. Turn work RS out so that picot-trimmed edge is on the outside. Set aside.

FINISHED SIZE
About 12" (30.5 cm) diameter and 6" (15 cm) deep, excluding handle.

YARN
Chunky weight (#5 Bulky).

Shown here: GGH Goa (50% cotton, 50% acrylic; 66 yd [60 m]/50 g): #17 light green, 8 balls.

NEEDLES
Size 9 (5.5 mm): 24" (60 cm) circular (cir) and set of 5 double-pointed (dpn). One smaller dpn and 1 smaller cir needle for picot edging. Adjust needle size if necessary to obtain the correct gauge.

NOTIONS
Size F/5 (3.75 mm) crochet hook; waste yarn; removable markers (m); tapestry needle; ¾ yd (0.75 meter) fabric for lining; two 12" (30.5 cm) diameter circles of plastic needlepoint canvas; two 8" (20.5 cm) zippers; sewing needle and matching thread.

GAUGE
15 stitches and 22 rounds = 4" (10 cm) in stockinette stitch worked in the round.

FRONT

With dpn, CO 8 sts. Distribute sts evenly on 4 dpn, place marker (pm), and join for working in the rnd, being careful not to twist sts. Work Rows 1–29 of Doily chart, changing to cir needle when there are enough sts to do so—160 sts; 8 sections of 20 sts each. Work picot-trimmed edge as foll: Work 3 rnds in St st. *Picot rnd:* *K2tog, yo; rep from * around. Work 3 rnds in St st. Place each purl bump from WS of first row of St st 7 rows below onto smaller cir needle, fold work along picot row so that purl sides of picot edge face tog and so that smaller cir needle is parallel to and behind working needle. Knit 1 row, working the sts from the two needles tog as if to k2tog—still 160 sts.

Inner Side

This is the point at which one end of the handle will be attached to the purse. Designate a top/center of the front and position RS of handle on RS of top/center. Knit to 9 sts before top/center. Hold one short edge of the handle in front of the needle with the public side (i.e., the side without the seam) of the handle facing the RS of the bag front. Use a crochet hook to pull the next 18 sts of the bag front evenly spaced through the edge of the handle and onto the spare dpn as shown at right. Cont with the yarn attached, knit these 18 sts, then knit to end of rnd. Rep this process on the next rnd to attach the WS of the handle (the side with the seam) in the same way, pulling sts through from the inside to the outside of the handle. Cont even in St st for 13 rnds. Place sts on waste yarn.

Think outside the box for innovative bag construction.

Doily

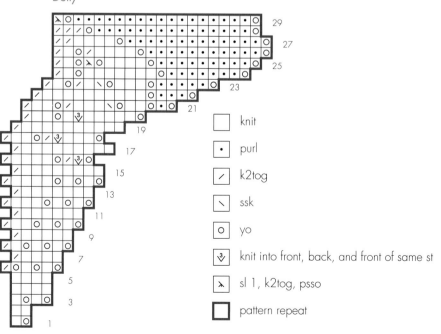

	knit
•	purl
╱	k2tog
╲	ssk
○	yo
⅋	knit into front, back, and front of same st
⋏	sl 1, k2tog, psso
	pattern repeat

BACK

CO 8 sts and work as for front.

JOIN FRONT AND BACK

Place markers 24 sts from each side of top/center point on front. CO 3 sts. Work I-cord BO (see Glossary, page 119) over these sts (which will conceal the zipper when it is closed)—112 sts rem. Rep for back. With RS tog, use the three-needle method to BO rem sts.

FINISHING

Weave in loose ends.

Lining

Using plastic canvas circles as a guide, cut two 13" (33 cm) diameter circles of lining fabric. Cut two 4" x 17" (10 x 43 cm) rectangles of lining fabric for attaching zippers. Fold under ½" (1.3 cm) seam allowance along one long edge of each lining rectangle and baste in place. Position zippers on top so that, when closed, the zipper pulls meet each other at the center, overlapping top edges of zipper tape as necessary. Zipper teeth should lie between rectangles, along fold of seam allowance. With WS of zippers facing WS of lining rectangles, hand sew zippers to lining rectangles. Cut a rectangle of lining fabric 7" (18 cm) wide by 26" (66 cm) long. With RS tog, sew short end of rectangle to short end of zipper/lining unit. With RS tog and leaving ½" (1.3 cm) free at zipper end, sew rectangle to edge of one lining circle. Sew to second circle in same manner. Seam short ends of rectangle. Insert plastic canvas circles into bag. With sewing needle and matching thread, sew WS of lining to inside of bag, centering zippers under I-cord BO. To stabilize each paisley point on the outer edges of the sides, use matching thread to sew each paisley point to the lining.

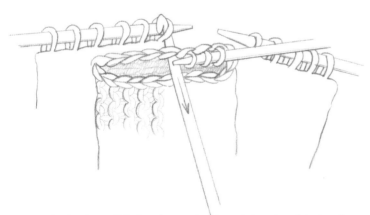

Use a crochet hook to pull the bag front stiches through the edge of the handle.

Circles cut from plastic needlepoint canvas help the purse keep its shape.

Laura Irwin used buttons and bobbles to decorate this sturdy bag. She began by knitting a rectangular base with the yarn doubled for extra thickness, then she picked up stitches around all four edges and worked the body of the bag to the top, using just a single strand of yarn. Along the way, she worked decreases to give the bag a graceful pouch shape. She added short tabs to the top of each side for attaching metal rings that secure the metal chain handle. To make a dense fabric that will keep its shape without an additional lining, Laura felted the bag in her washing machine. For added interest, she knitted a single stockinette-stitch panel that she decorated with bobbles and buttons and attached to the center of the bag front, base, and back.

STITCH GUIDE

Make Bobble (MB)
(K1, p1, k1, p1) into same st; pass 2nd, 3rd, and 4th sts over the first.

BAG

With 2 strands of yarn held tog and largest needles, CO 34 sts.

Base

Beg with a RS row, work in St st for 12 rows, ending with a WS row.

Sides

(RS) K34, place marker (pm), pick up and knit 11 sts along short side of piece already knitted, pm, pick up and knit 34 sts along CO edge, pm, pick up and knit 11 sts along other short side, pm of unique color—90 sts total. Join for working in the rnd. Knit 21 rnds. Change to a single strand of yarn and middle-size needles. Knit 12 rnds. *Dec rnd:* Ssk, knit to 2 sts before m, k2tog, slip marker (sl m), k11, sl m, ssk, knit to 2 sts before m, k2tog, sl m, k11—4 sts dec'd. Rep Dec rnd once more—82 sts rem. Knit 26 rnds. *Next rnd:* BO 30 sts, k11 for ring strap and place these 11 sts on a holder, BO 30 sts, k11 for other ring strap.

Ring Straps

Work 11 sts back and forth in St st for 9 rows. BO all sts. Rejoin yarn to 11 held ring strap sts and work in St st for 9 rows. BO all sts.

FINISHED SIZE
About 14½" (37 cm) wide at base, 10½" (26.5 cm) wide at top, and 12" (30.5 cm) long after felting.

YARN
Worsted weight (#4 Medium).
Shown here: Tahki Donegal Tweed Homespun (100% wool; 183 yd [167 m]/100 g): #866 grey tweed, 3 skeins.

NEEDLES
Sizes 13 (9 mm) and 11 (8 mm): 20" (50 cm) circular (cir); size 8 (5 mm). Adjust needle size if necessary to obtain the correct gauge.

NOTIONS
Markers, one of a unique color (m); stitch holder; tapestry needle; two 1½" (3.8 cm) silver rings (rings shown are item #4804 by La Mode); 20" (51 cm) heavy chain (www.davabeadandtrade.com); 2 sets of pliers; sharp-point sewing needle and matching thread; lingerie bag; twelve ⅞" (2.2 cm) half-ball covered buttons; four 1⅛" (3 cm) half-ball covered buttons; ⅛ yd (0.15 meter) fabric for button covers.

GAUGE
12½ stitches and 16¾ rows = 4" (10 cm) with single strand of yarn in stockinette stitch on middle-size needles, before felting. 10½ stitches and 13½ rows = 4" (10 cm) with double strand of yarn in stockinette stitch on largest needles, before felting.

A metal chain makes a strong and flexible strap.

UNFELTED BOBBLE PANEL

With a single strand of yarn and smallest needles, CO 29 sts.

Row 1: (RS) K4, p2, MB (see Stitch Guide), p1, k13, p1, MB, p2, k4.

Row 2 and all WS rows: Knit the knits and purl the purls.

Row 3: K4, p2, k1, p1, k13, p1, k1, p2, k4.

Rows 5–12: Rep Rows 1–4 two times.

Rows 13 and 14: Rep Rows 3 and 4.

Rep Rows 1–14 three more times—piece measures 9¼" (23.5 cm) from CO. Rep Rows 1–4 eight times, then work Rows 3 and 4 once—piece measures 14¾" (37.5 cm) from CO. Rep Rows 1–14 three more times, then work Rows 1–4 two times, then work Row 1 once more—piece measures 23½" (59.5 cm) from CO. With WS facing, BO all sts in patt.

FINISHING

Weave in loose ends.

Felting

Fold ring strap over ring and whipstitch (see Glossary, page 124) to inside of bag. Place bag in lingerie bag and put in washing machine set for shortest cycle with lowest water level and hottest water. Add a little laundry soap and a pair of blue jeans to help agitation. Do not let bag go through the rinse cycle. Check progress every 5 minutes; it may take several cycles to felt to the desired thickness. Squeeze out water and roll in a bath towel to remove excess moisture. Lay flat and pull into shape. Let air-dry completely.

Blocking

Block unfelted panel with damp towel and warm iron.

Attach Panel to Bag

Center unfelted panel along center of felted bag, aligning CO edge of panel with top edge of bag front and BO edge of panel with top edge of bag back. With sewing needle and matching thread, sew panel in place using a backstitch (see Glossary, page 124), leaving top edge open for pocket, if desired.

Buttons

Cover buttons with fabric according to directions on button package. With sewing needle and matching thread, sew buttons onto unfelted panel, catching the felted fabric for stability. Sew smaller buttons next to 2nd, 5th, and 8th bobble from top of panel, and larger buttons next to 11th bobble from top of panel.

Attach Strap

Using pliers, open ring and slip end of chain onto ring. Close ring.

In true yoga fashion, **Sharon O'Brien** combined elements of calm (Van Gogh "stars" on a "sky" of cool, deep teal) and energy (warm vibrant stripes) in this bag designed to carry a yoga mat. Sharon worked the square base in garter stitch at a tight gauge, then picked up stitches around the base and worked the body in stockinette stitch to the top. She added false seam stitches at the corners and eyelets for a drawstring at the top. To reinforce the drawstring eyelets, Sharon sewed crocheted circles around each hole. For the strap, she knitted a wide stockinette strap that she allowed to curl in on itself naturally.

BASE

With MC, smaller needles, crochet hook, and using the chain-edge method (see Glossary, page 119), CO 34 sts. Work even in garter st (knit every row) until there are 34 garter ridges on one side of the fabric and 33 ridges on the other. Loosely BO all sts but do not fasten off last st. Do not cut yarn. Place last st on larger 16" (40 cm) cir needle. With RS facing, pick up and knit 33 sts along side of base, place marker (pm), [pick up and knit 34 sts along next side, pm] 3 times, using unique-colored m for last rep to denote end of rnd—136 sts total.

BODY

Inc rnd: P1, M1 (see Glossary, page 123), *knit to next m, M1, slip marker (sl m), p1, M1; rep from * 2 more times, knit to end-of-rnd m, M1, sl m—144 sts; 1 purl st at each corner and 1 st inc'd each side of each purl st. Change to longer cir needle. Work 1 rnd even in St st, purling corner sts as established. Rep Inc rnd—152 sts. Maintaining purl sts as established, work stripe patt as foll: [3 rnds pale celery, 5 rnds burnt orange, 3 rnds aqua, 2 rnds lilac, 3 rnds burgundy, 5 rnds acid green, 3 rnds teal] 3 times, 3 rnds pale celery, 5 rnds burnt orange, 3 rnds aqua, 2 rnds lilac, 3 rnds burgundy—piece measures about 12¼" (31 cm) from base. Change to teal and cont even in St st with 1 purl st at each corner until piece measures about 12¼" (31 cm) from last color change.

FINISHED SIZE
About 26½" (67.5 cm) around and 27" (68.5 cm) long.

YARN
Worsted weight (#4 Medium).

Shown here: Tahki Cotton Classic (100% mercerized cotton; 108 yd [99 m]/50 g): #3786 teal (MC), 6 skeins; #3715 acid green, #3712 pale celery, #3407 burnt orange, #3800 aqua, #3936 lilac, and #3432 burgundy, 1 skein each.

NEEDLES
Body—size 5 (3.75 mm): 16" and 24" (40 and 60 cm) circular (cir). Base—size 3 (3.25 mm). Adjust needle size if necessary to obtain the correct gauge.

NOTIONS
Size F/5 (3.75 mm) crochet hook; markers (m), one of a unique color; large tapestry needle; DMC 6-strand embroidery floss in #209 lilac, #472 celery, #920 burnt orange, and #3846 aqua; size 22 tapestry needle for embroidery; tracing paper (optional); straight pins (optional).

GAUGE
23 stitches and 30 rounds = 4" (10 cm) in stockinette stitch on larger needles.

Upper Band

Cut teal and join burnt orange. *Next rnd:* K2tog, k73, k2tog, knit to end of rnd—150 sts rem. Remove all but end-of-rnd marker. Purl 1 rnd. Cut orange and join acid green. Knit 3 rnds. *Eyelet rnd:* K10, *k2tog, [yo] 2 times, ssk, k21; rep from *, ending last rep k11—6 eyelets. *Next rnd:* Knit, working k1, p1 in each double yo of previous rnd. Knit 3 rnds. Cut acid green and join burnt orange. Knit 1 rnd, purl 1 rnd. Cut burnt orange and join teal. *Dec rnd:* K37, k2tog, k74, k2tog, knit to end of rnd—148 sts rem. Work in garter st (purl 1 rnd, knit 1 rnd) for 9 rnds. Loosely BO all sts.

STRAP

With MC and larger needle, CO 23 sts. Do not join. Working back and forth in rows, knit 2 rows.
Row 3: Ssk, k9, M1, k1, M1, k9, k2tog.
Rows 4–6: Knit.
Rep Rows 3–6 four more times. *Dec row:* Ssk, k19, k2tog—21 sts rem. Beg with a WS row, work even in St st until piece measures 22" (56 cm) from dec row, ending with a WS row. *Inc row:* K1, M1, k19, M1, k1—23 sts. Work even in garter st for 4¼" (11 cm). Loosely BO all sts, leaving a 10" (25.5 cm) tail to use later to attach strap to bag.

Crocheted circles make colorful "grommets."

DRAWSTRING

With MC and larger needle, CO 3 sts. Work 3-st I-cord (see Glossary, page 124) until piece measures 38" (96.5 cm). BO all sts.

CROCHET CIRCLES (MAKE 6)

With burnt orange and crochet hook (see Glossary, page 120, for crochet instructions), ch 7, join with a sl st to form ring. Ch 2, work 16 hdc into ring, and join with sl st into top of beg ch-2. Fasten off. Cut yarn, leaving a 10" (25.5 cm) tail to use later to attach circle to bag.

FINISHING

Weave in loose ends. Sew crochet circles around eyelets on upper band of bag body.

Embroidery

Draw free-form spirals onto small circles of tracing paper. Pin paper circles to solid-colored area of bag as desired. With 3 strands of DMC color of your choice threaded on a tapestry needle, work split-st embroidery (see Glossary, page 122) along motif, being careful not to pull sts so tight as to cause puckers. Hold embroidered stitches down with thumb as you carefully tear away tracing paper. Remove bits of paper caught under embroidery sts with tweezers. Repeat for other spirals as desired.

Strap

Allow St st area of strap to roll naturally until the edges touch each other. With MC threaded on a tapestry needle, use the mattress st (see Glossary, page 124) to sew the edges tog for 12" (30.5 cm) along center of strap. Center lower edge of strap over the purl st that denotes beg of rnd and sew to edge of garter st base. Sew top edge of strap to upper edge of bag.

Insert I-cord drawstring through eyelets so that ends of I-cord are opposite the strap.

Frustrated by the inconvenience of carrying her iPod around in her hand, **Ann Budd** set out to knit a portable iPod case. She knitted the pocket in the round from the base up, working simple two-stitch cables (that don't require a cable needle) on the front and a single rib on the back to make the pocket hug the iPod snugly. When seaming the base, Ann left a small hole to accommodate the earphone jack. She finished the case off with a cabled knit-cord neck strap that extends along the sides of the pocket. There's even a handy little strap across the back of the pocket to corral the earphone cables.

STITCH GUIDE

LT (worked over 2 sts)
Skip first st on left needle, take right needle to far side of fabric and knit second st through the back loop, then knit the first st and slip both sts off needle.

RT (worked over 2 sts)
K2tog but do not slip sts off left needle, knit the first st again, then slip both sts off needle.

BAG

CO 31 sts. Arrange sts on 3 dpn, place marker (pm), and join for working in the rnd, being careful not to twist sts.

Rnd 1: K3 (bag side), pm, [p1, k1] 6 times, p1 (bag back), pm, k3 (bag side), pm, k12 (bag front). Slip markers every rnd.

Rnd 2: Sl 1, k1, sl 1, [p1, k1] 6 times, p1, sl 1, k1, sl 1, [LT (see Stitch Guide), RT (see Stitch Guide)] 3 times.

Rep these 2 rnds 18 more times—piece measures about 4" (10 cm) from CO. Work I-cord BO as foll: Use the backward-loop method (see Glossary, page 119) to CO 2 sts. *Sl 2 sts to left needle, k1, k2tog; rep from * until no sts rem on left needle. Lift the first st on right needle over second st and off the needle—1 st rem. Cut yarn, pull on rem st until cut end comes through st to secure.

FINISHED SIZE
About 2" (5 cm) wide, 4" (10 cm) tall (excluding handle), and ½" (1.3 cm) deep.

YARN
Sportweight (#2 Fine).
Shown here: Zitron Samoa (100% cotton; 115 yd [105 m]/50 g): #86 tangerine, 1 ball.

NEEDLES
Size 3 (3.25 mm): Set of 4 double-pointed (dpn). Adjust needle size if necessary to obtain the correct gauge.

NOTIONS
Markers (m); tapestry needle; cable needle.

GAUGE
28 stitches and 40 rows = 4" (10 cm) in stockinette stitch.

Corral the earphone cables in the handy little strap across the back.

FINISHING

With yarn threaded on a tapestry needle, sew base of bag, leaving about ½" (1.3 cm) open at right edge for earphone cable.

Neck Strap

CO 5 sts. Do not turn, but slide sts to opposite end of needle and pull yarn across back in position to work another RS row. Work I-cord (see Glossary, page 124) as foll, always working with RS facing:

Rows 1–3: K5, slide sts to opposite end of needle and pull yarn across back in position to work another RS row.

Row 4: K1, sl 1 onto cable needle and hold in front, k2, k1 from cable needle, k1, slide sts to opposite end of needle.

Rep Rows 1–4 until strap measures 34" (86.5 cm), or desired length. BO all sts. With yarn threaded on a tapestry needle and beg at base of bag, sew strap to both sides of bag along the 3-st sides (denoted by slipped sts), being careful not to twist strap.

Cable Strap

Measure 1½" (3.8 cm) up from bottom seam on back and mark for cable strap placement. With RS facing, pick up and knit 3 sts along side edge of back at marked position. Work as foll:

Row 1: (WS) P1, k1, p1.

Row 2: (RS) K1, p1, k1.

Rep these 2 rows until piece measures about 1¾" (4.5 cm) and fits across back when stretched. BO all sts. Sew BO edge of strap to other side edge of back at marked position. Weave in loose ends.

Don't have a pocket?
Knit your own!

Circles of color play against each other all around this colorful drawstring bag. Designer Judith L. Swartz worked a circular base, then joined fifty-two separate medallions to create the tall sides. For simplicity, Judith worked all the medallions the same way but varied the color sequences for an exciting visual composition. She finished off the bag with rounds of single crochet punctuated with eyelets to accommodate an I-cord drawstring. Then she attached a crocheted handle to the drawstring. To keep contents from poking out between the medallions, Judith lined the bag with cotton fabric.

STITCH GUIDE

Yo-Yo Color Sequence

Beginning with the first color listed, work yo-yos (see page 78) as follows:

Motif 1: (make 6) E, A, D.
Motif 2: (make 6) B, E, A.
Motif 3: (make 5) C, D, E.
Motif 4: (make 5) A, E, B.
Motif 5: (make 5) B, A, C.
Motif 6: (make 5) A, C, D.
Motif 7: (make 5) C, B, A.
Motif 8: (make 5) B, A, E.
Motif 9: (make 5) D, C, B.
Motif 10: (make 5) E, B, C.

FINISHED SIZE

About 23" (58.5 cm) in circumference and 12½" (31.5 cm) tall.

YARN

DK weight (#3 Light).

Shown here: GGH Scarlett (100% mercerized cotton; 120 yd [110 m]/50 g): #9 raspberry (A), 3 balls; #10 terra-cotta (B), #30 light pink (C), #12 pale peach (D), and #8 wine (E), 1 ball each.

HOOK

Size D/3 (3.25 mm). Adjust hook size if necessary to obtain the correct gauge.

NOTIONS

Tapestry needle; ½ yd (0.5 m) cotton fabric for lining; sharp-point sewing needle and matching thread; sewing pins.

GAUGE

26 stitches and 28 rounds = 4" (10 cm) in single crochet.

YO-YOS

Using colors as specified (see Stitch Guide), make 52 yo-yo motifs as foll: With first color, ch 4, join with sl st to form ring. Cont in rnds as foll:

Rnd 1: Ch 1, work 10 sc in ring, join with sl st to beg sc. Fasten off first color.

Rnd 2: Attach second color, ch 1, work 2 sc in each sc, join with sl st to beg sc—20 sc. Fasten off second color.

Rnd 3: Attach third color, ch 1, *work 2 sc in first sc, work 1 sc in next sc; rep from *, join with sl st to beg sc—30 sc. Fasten off third color.

JOIN YO-YOS

Referring to illustrations below for motif placement and reading chart in columns from top to bottom, join motifs by columns as foll.

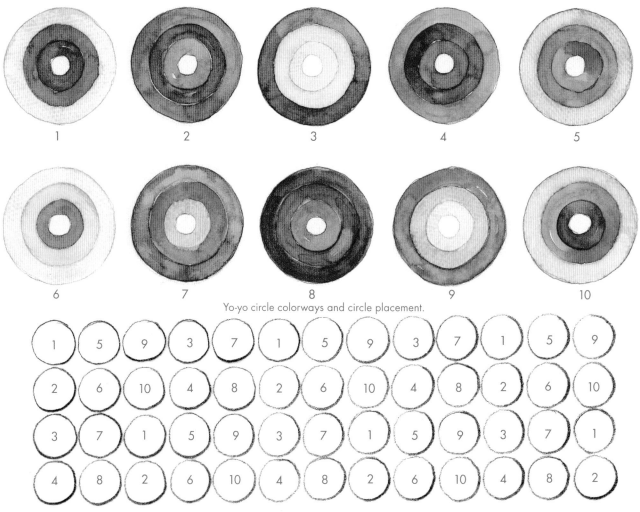

Yo-yo circle colorways and circle placement.

Column 1

Attach A to first motif, ch 1, work 1 sc in each of first 7 sc, ch 2, work 1 sc in each of next 8 sc, ch 1, attach A to second motif, work 1 sc in same sc, work 1 sc in each of next 6 sc, ch 2, work 1 sc in each of next 8 sc, ch 1, attach A to third motif, work 1 sc in same sc, work 1 sc in each of next 6 sc, ch 2, work 1 sc in each of next 8 sc, ch 1, attach A to fourth motif, work 1 sc in same sc, work 1 sc in each of next 6 sc, ch 2, work 1 sc in each of next 8 sc, ch 2 (bottom of column), * work 1 sc in each of next 7 sc, ch 2, work 1 sc in each of next 8 sc, work 1 sc in first sc (you now have 2 sc in this sc to complete circle), work 1 sc in ch 1 between motifs*, move up to next motif and rep from * to * 3 more times, ending top motif by working ch 2 before joining to beg sc.

Columns 2–12

Work as for column 1, but instead of working ch 2 on first side of motif, work (ch 1, ch 1 through ch-2 of corresponding motif of previous column) to join. Work second side of column the same as first column.

Column 13

Work first side as for columns 2–12, work second side of column as for first, joining column 13 to column 1.

What can you
do with fifty-two
crocheted medallions?

BASE

With A, ch 4, join with sl st to form ring.

Rnd 1: Ch 1, work 10 sc into ring, join with sl st to beg sc—10 sc.

Rnd 2: Ch 1, work 2 sc in each sc, join with sl st to beg sc—20 sc.

Fasten off A and join B.

Rnd 3: Ch 1, *work 1 sc in first sc, work 2 sc in next sc; rep from *, join with sl st to beg sc—30 sc.

Rnd 4: Ch 1, *work 2 sc in first sc, work 1 sc in each of next 2 sc; rep from *, join with sl st to beg sc—40 sc.

Fasten off B and join C.

Rnd 5: Ch 1, *work 2 sc in first sc, work 1 sc in each of next 3 sc; rep from *, join with sl st to beg sc—50 sc.

Fasten off C and join D.

Rnd 6: Ch 1, work 1 sc in each sc, join with sl st to beg sc.

Fasten off D and join B.

Rnd 7: Ch 1, *work 2 sc in first sc, work 1 sc in each of next 4 sc; rep from *, join with sl st to beg sc—60 sc.

Fasten off B and join E.

Rnd 8: Ch 1, work 1 sc in each sc, join with sl st to beg sc.

Rnd 9: Ch 1, *work 2 sc in first sc, work 1 sc in each of next 5 sc; rep from *, join with sl st to beg sc—70 sc.

Fasten off E and join A.

Rnd 10: Ch 1, work 1 sc in each sc, join with sl st to beg sc.

Fasten off A and join C.

Rnd 11: Ch 1, *work 2 sc in first sc, work 1 sc in each of next 6 sc; rep from *, join with sl st to beg sc—80 sc.

Rnd 12: Ch 1, work 1 sc in each sc, join with sl st to beg sc.

Fasten off C and join A.

Rnd 13: Ch 1, *work 2 sc in first sc, work 1 sc in each of next 7 sc; rep from *, join with sl st to beg sc—90 sc.

Rnd 14: Ch 1, work 1 sc in each sc, join with sl st to beg sc.

Rnd 15: Ch 1, *work 2 sc in first sc, work 1 sc in each of next 8 sc; rep from *, join with sl st to beg sc—100 sc.

Fasten off A and join D.

Rnd 16: Ch 1, *work 2 sc in first sc, work 1 sc in each of next 9 sc; rep from *, join with sl st to beg sc—110 sc.

Rnd 17: Ch 1, work 1 sc in each sc, join with sl st to beg sc.

Fasten off D and join B.

Rnd 18: Ch 1, *work 2 sc in first sc, work 1 sc in each of next 10 sc; rep from *, join with sl st to beg sc—120 sc.

Rnd 19: Ch 1, *work 2 sc in first sc, work 1 sc in each of next 11 sc; rep from *, join with sl st to beg sc—130 sc.

Fasten off B and join E.

Rnd 20: Ch 1, work 1 sc in each sc, join with sl st to beg sc.

Fasten off E and join C.

Rnd 21: Ch 1, *work 2 sc in first sc, work 1 sc in each of next 12 sc; rep from *, join with sl st to beg sc—140 sc.

Rnd 22: Ch 1, work 1 sc in each sc, join with sl st to beg sc.

Fasten off C and join A.

Rnd 23: Ch 1, *work 2 sc in first sc, work 1 sc in each of next 13 sc; rep from *, join with sl st to beg sc—150 sc.

Rnds 24 and 25: Ch 1, work 1 sc in each sc, join with sl st to beg sc.

Rnd 26: (turning line) Ch 1, work 1 sl st into back loop only of each sc.

Rnd 27: Ch 1, work 1 sc in each sl st, join with sl st to beg sc.

Rnds 28 and 29: Ch 1, work 1 sc in each sc, join with sl st to beg sc.

Fasten off A and join C.

Rnd 30: Ch 1, work 1 sc in each sc, join with sl st to beg sc.

Fasten off C and join B.

Rnd 31: Ch 1, work 1 sc in each sc, join with sl st to beg sc.

Fasten off B and join A.

Rnds 32 and 33: Ch 1, work 1 sc in each sc, join with sl st to beg sc.

Fasten off A and join E.

Rnd 34: Ch 1, work 1 sc in each sc, join with sl st to beg sc.

Fasten off E and join A.

Rnds 35 and 36: Ch 1, work 1 sc in each sc, join with sl st to beg sc.

A woven cotton lining keeps the contents secure.

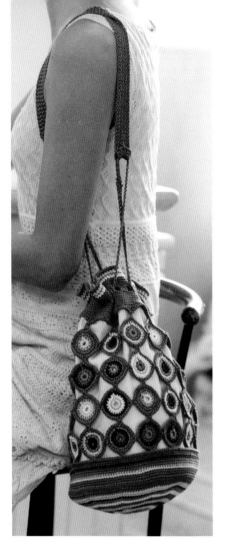

Follow the color
sequences shown
here or let serendipity
be your guide.

JOIN YO-YOS TO BASE

Cont with A, ch 1, *work 1 sc in each of first 12 sc, work 1 sl st through bottom ch-2 loop of first column of yo-yos, work 1 sc in each of next 11 sc, work 1 sl st through bottom ch-2 loop of next yo-yo column; rep from * to last 12 sc, work 1 sc in each of next 12 sc, work 1 sl st through bottom ch-2 loop of last column of yo-yos, join with sl st to beg sc. Fasten off.

TOP

Join A to top ch-2 loop of first yo-yo, ch 1, work 1 sc in same loop, *ch 10, work 1 sc in top ch-2 loop of next yo-yo column, ch 11, work 1 sc in top ch-2 loop of next yo-yo column; rep from * 5 more times, ch 11, join with sl st to beg sc. Cont in rnds as foll:

Rnd 1: Ch 1, work 1 sc in first sc, *work 1 sc in each of next 10 ch, work 1 sc in next sc, work 1 sc in each of next 11 ch, work 1 sc in next sc; rep from * 5 more times, work 1 sc in each of next 11 ch, join with sl st to beg sc—150 sc.

Rnd 2: Ch 1, work 1 sc in each sc, join with sl st to beg sc.

Rnds 3–8: Rep Rnd 2.

Rnd 9: (drawstring eyelet rnd) Ch 3, work 1 dc in each of next 2 sc, *ch 2, skip next 2 sc, work 1 dc in each of next 3 sc; rep from * to last 2 sc, ch 2, skip last 2 sc, join with sl st to top of beg ch-3—30 ch-2 spaces.

Rnd 10: Ch 1, work 1 sc in each st and 2 sc in each space around, join with sl st to beg sc—150 sc.

Rnds 11, 12, and 13: Rep Rnd 2.

Fasten off A and join D.

Rnd 14: Rep Rnd 2.

Fasten off D and join B.

Rnd 15: Rep Rnd 2.

Fasten off B and join C.

Rnd 16: Rep Rnd 2.

Fasten off C and join A.

Rnds 17 and 18: Rep Rnd 2.

Rnd 19: Ch 1, work reverse single crochet in each sc, join with sl st to beg sc. Fasten off.

DRAWSTRING

With A, ch 171. Work 1 sc in 2nd ch from hook and in each ch across—170 sc. Fasten off.

HANDLE

With A, ch 97.

Row 1: Work 1 sc in 2nd ch from hook and in each ch across, turn—96 sc.

Rows 2–8: Ch 1, work 1 sc in each sc, turn.

Fasten off.

FINISHING

Thread drawstring through eyelets. With A threaded on a tapestry needle, sew ends of drawstring tog securely. Fold under ½" (1.3 cm) on one short edge of handle, slide over drawstring at side of bag, and sew end of handle in place, keeping drawstring free, as shown below. Rep for other end of handle. Weave in loose ends.

Lining

Cut a circle of lining fabric 9" (23 cm) in diameter for bottom of lining. Cut a rectangle of lining fabric 10¾" (27.5 cm) wide by 25" (63.5 cm) long. With WS of lining fabric tog, sew short edges tog with a ¼" (6 mm) seam. Turn WS out and sew seam again with a $^3/_8$" (1 cm) seam allowance, encasing original seam allowances. For ease in attaching tube to circle, sew a line ½" (1.3 cm) from bottom end of tube and clip at even intervals close to stitching line. With RS tog, pin tube to circle, easing to fit, and sew tog ½" (1.3 cm) from edge. Turn under ½" (1.3 cm) at upper edge of tube and press. Insert lining into bag. Whipstitch (see Glossary, page 124) lining to upper edge of WS of bag, below drawstring.

The handle is sewn to the drawstring, which closes the bag when you pick it up.

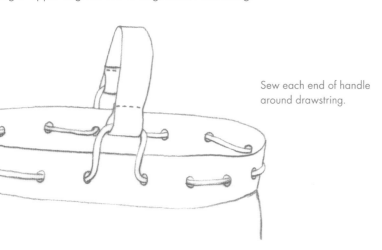

Sew each end of handle around drawstring.

CELTIC WEEKEND TOTE
LISA B. EVANS

Knitted from soft Rowan Scottish Tweed, Lisa B. Evans's tote is a welcome companion on a weekend away. A colorful chunky Fair Isle pattern, made more dynamic by Lisa's technique of changing pattern and background at wide intervals on different rows, makes a striking design on the bag's front and back. For a roomy bag, Lisa worked a separate ribbed gusset that extends seamlessly into the shoulder strap. She added a matching buttonhole tab and a large button for fastening and lined the inside with contrasting woven fabric.

NOTE
✤ All DK-weight yarn is used double throughout.

FRONT

With MC (doubled), larger needles, and using the long-tail method (see Glossary, page 120), CO 66 sts. *Next row:* (RS) Sl 1 (selvedge st), work Row 1 of Celtic chart across 64 sts, k1 (selvedge st). Slip the first st and knit last st of every row, work center 64 sts according to Rows 2–80 of chart, working medallions in intarsia and other color work in Fair Isle method—piece measures 16¾" (42.5 cm) from CO.

Facing
With yellow-green, cont even in St st for 2½" (6.5 cm) more. BO all sts.

FINISHED SIZE
About 16½" (42 cm) wide, 16¾" (42.5 cm) tall, and 6" (15 cm) deep.

YARN
DK and chunky weight (#3 Light and #5 Bulky).

Shown here: Rowan Scottish Tweed DK (100% pure new wool; 124 yd [113 m]/ 50 g): #22 Celtic mix (dark green; MC), 8 balls; #19 peat (dark brown), #15 apple (yellow-green), #11 sunset (orange-red), #17 lobster (deep red), #31 indigo, #18 thatch (yellow-brown), 2 balls each; #25 oatmeal, 1 ball.

Rowan Scottish Tweed Chunky (100% pure new wool; 109 yd [100 m]/100 g): #6 sea green (light blue), 2 balls.

NEEDLES
Body—size 9 (5.5 mm); ribbing—size 8 (5 mm). Adjust needle size if necessary to obtain the correct gauge.

NOTIONS
Stitch holders; about 1 yd (1 m) waste yarn; tapestry needle; sewing needle and matching thread; 40" x 22" (101.5 x 56 cm) lining fabric; two 2" (5 cm) buttons.

GAUGE
16 stitches and 19 rows = 4" (10 cm) in charted pattern on larger needles with DK yarn used double or chunky yarn used single. *Note:* Exact gauge is not as important as consistent, firm fabric.

Celtic

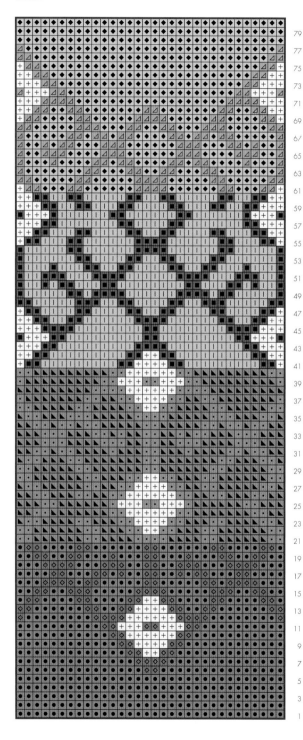

- ● dark green (MC)
- ◇ deep red
- ◤ indigo
- ∙ dark brown
- + oatmeal
- I light blue
- ▣ orange-red
- ◆ yellow-green
- ◿ yellow-brown

BACK

Work as for front.

GUSSET

With MC doubled, waste yarn, smaller needles, and using the invisible method (see Glossary, page 120), provisionally CO 36 sts.
Row 1: (RS) Sl 1, *k2, p2; rep from * to last 3 sts, k3.
Row 2: Sl 1, *p2, k2; rep from * to last 3 sts, p2, k1.
Rep Rows 1 and 2 until piece measures 85" (216 cm) from CO. Place sts on holder.

TAB

With MC doubled and smaller needles, CO 14 sts.
Row 1: (RS) Sl 1, k1, *p2, k2; rep from * to end of row.
Row 2: Sl 1, p1, *k2, p2; rep from * to end of row.
Rep Rows 1 and 2 until piece measures 5½" (14 cm) from CO. *Next row:* Work 7 sts in patt and place these sts on holder, work in patt to end of row—7 sts rem. Cont in rib as established for 7 rows. Place these 7 sts on holder and work first 7 sts to match.
Next row: Work across all 14 sts in rib as established. Cont in rib until piece measures 2" (5 cm) from joining row. BO all sts in patt and *at the same time,* dec by working k2tog above each pair of knit sts and p2tog above each pair of purl sts.

FINISHING

Block front and back with damp towel and warm iron.

Seams

With MC threaded on a tapestry needle, RS tog, and beg about 1" (2.5 cm) from start of gusset, sew gusset to side and bottom edges of front, leaving facing free and pulling gusset slightly. Sew other edge of gusset to back. Sew extra sts securely at corners where gusset and front/back meet. Fold facing to inside and sew sides in place to cover seams, leaving lower edge of facing free. Remove waste yarn from provisional CO of gusset and place live sts on smaller needle. Use the three-needle method (see Glossary, page 119) to BO the sts tog or use MC threaded on a tapestry needle and the Kitchener st for ribbing (see Glossary, page 122) to graft the sts tog.

Tab

Center tab over top opening and sew non-buttonhole end in place about 3" (7.5 cm) down from top edge of back. Sew button to front opposite buttonhole, allowing about 2" (5 cm) gap at top. Sew second button to back tab opposite front button.

Lining

Fold lining in half widthwise and sew sides tog. Press side seams open. Fold up bottom corner to WS about 3" (7.5 cm) and sew across point to hold in place. Measure finished depth of bag to lower edge of facing. Fold top edge of lining down to just cover knitted facing edge and press fold in place. Place lining inside bag with WS tog and sew to lower edge of facings by hand or machine, leaving lining loose along gussets (but sew along fold of lining to prevent raveling). *Note:* If sewing lining by machine, leave about 6" (15 cm) of one side seam open.

After sewing lining in place along facings, pull up the side seam at the gusset and sew closed.

Make a seamless strap by extending the gusset.

Mary Jane Mucklestone took the earflap on a traditional chullo hat of the Andes, blew the design up, and made it into a playful bag. She began by knitting a strip of colorful garter-stitch squares and triangles for the outer edge of the bag front and back, then she picked up stitches along the top edge and worked paired double decreases in another stripe pattern to shape the strips into oversize "earflaps." She joined the front and back to a shaped garter-stitch gusset that continues from the top edge to form the shoulder strap. A row of single crochet prevents the top edge from stretching, and a chain-stitch loop and toggle button make a snappy closure.

FRONT

Outer Strip

With dpn and orange, CO 8 sts. Do not join into a rnd. Knit 12 rows with each of the foll colors: orange, teal, natural, chartreuse, red—60 rows total.

First Corner

With orange, work short-rows as foll:
Rows 1–4: Knit.
Row 5: K7, turn, sl 1, k6.
Row 6: K6, turn, sl 1, k5.
Row 7: K5, turn, sl 1, k4.
Row 8: K4, turn, sl 1, k3.
Row 9: K3, turn, sl 1, k2.
Row 10: K2, turn, sl 1, k1.
With teal, knit 12 rows. With natural, knit 12 rows.

Second Corner

With chartreuse, rep Rows 1–10 of first corner.
Knit 12 rows with each of the foll colors: red, orange, teal, natural, chartreuse. BO all sts.

FINISHED SIZE
About 12" (30.5 cm) wide, 11" (28 cm) tall, and 4" (10 cm) deep, excluding strap.

YARN
Bulky weight (#6 Super Bulky).
Shown here: Dale of Norway Hubro (100% wool; 36 yd [33 m]/50 g): #4227 red and #4636 fuchsia, 2 balls each; #3418 orange, #7062 teal, #0020 natural, and #9636 chartreuse, 1 ball each. *Note:* This bag uses up all of the yarn; purchase extra if you plan to make changes to the design.

NEEDLES
Size 10 (6 mm): set of 4 or 5 double-pointed (dpn) and 24" (60 cm) circular (cir). Adjust needle size if necessary to obtain the correct gauge.

NOTIONS
Size J/10 (6 mm) crochet hook; markers (m); tapestry needle; one 2¼" (5.5 cm) toggle button.

GAUGE
15 stitches and 28 rows = 4" (10 cm) in garter stitch.

Center

Row 1: With fuchsia, cir needle, and RS facing, pick up and knit 1 st for each garter ridge along shorter long edge of outer strip (30 sts total), place marker (pm), pick up and knit 2 sts at point of short-rowed corner, 6 sts after corner, pm, 6 sts before next corner, 2 sts at point of other short-rowed corner, pm, and 30 sts along rem side—76 sts total.

Row 2 and all WS rows: Knit, using same color as for previous row.

Row 3: With chartreuse, knit to 3 sts before first m, sl 1, k2tog, psso, slip marker (sl m), k8, sl m, k8, sl m, k3tog, knit to end of row—72 sts rem.

Row 5: With natural, knit to 3 sts before first m, sl 1, k2tog, psso, sl m, knit to 3 sts before next m, ssk, k1, sl m, k1, k2tog, knit to next m, sl m, k3tog, knit to end of row—6 sts dec'd.

Row 7: With orange, rep Row 5—60 sts rem.

Row 9: With red, rep Row 5—54 sts rem.

Rows 11 and 13: With fuchsia, rep Row 5—42 sts rem after Row 13.

Row 15: With teal, knit to 3 sts before first m, sl 1, k2tog, psso, sl m, ssk, k1, sl m, k1, k2tog, sl m, k3tog, knit to end of row—36 sts rem.

Row 17: With teal, knit to 3 sts before first m, sl 1, k2tog, psso, sl m, ssk, remove m, k2tog, sl m, k3tog, knit to end of row—30 sts rem.

Row 19: With teal, knit to 3 sts before first m, sl 1, k2tog, psso, sl m, k2, sl m, k3tog, knit to end of row—26 sts rem.

Row 20: Knit.

Divide sts evenly onto 2 needles—13 sts each needle. With RS tog, use the three-needle method (see Glossary, page 119), to BO rem sts tog.

BACK

Work as for front.

GUSSET PANEL

With red and dpn, CO 8 sts. With RS facing, pick up 1 loop from end of first garter ridge of bag front, place picked-up loop on left needle, and work it tog with next st on needle as k2tog, knit to last st, sl 1 kwise, pick up 1 loop from end of first garter ridge of bag back and place loop on right needle, work picked-up loop and sl st tog as for ssk. Knit 1 (WS) row. Rep the last 2 rows and *at the same time*, on (RS) rows 13, 19, 25, and 31, inc 1 st each end of row by working M1 (see Glossary, page 123) 1 st from each selvedge edge—2 sts inc'd on each of these rows; 16 sts after all shaping is complete. Work even on 16 sts, joining to bag front and back as established, until 62 rows have been worked from CO. Change to fuchsia and work even as established for 52 rows. Change to red and work even as established for 30 rows. Dec 1 st each end of needle on next row, then every foll 6th row 3 more times, working dec 1 st in from each selvedge edge—8 sts rem when all shaping is complete. Work even to top of bag. When the top of the bag is reached, with RS facing, pick up and knit 1 st from top of bag front, k8 gusset sts, then pick up and knit 1 st from top of bag back—10 sts total.

Strap

Slipping the first st of every row, knit 7 rows with red, ending with a WS row. With fuchsia, knit 32 rows. With orange, knit 40 rows. With fuchsia, knit 36 rows. With red, knit 6 rows. With red and a spare needle, pick up and knit 1 st from top of bag back, 8 sts from CO end of gusset panel, and 1 st from top of bag front—10 sts total on spare needle. With WS tog and being careful not to twist strap, use the three-needle method to BO rem sts tog.

FINISHING

With teal, crochet hook, RS facing, and beg at front opening edge, work single crochet (sc; see Glossary, page 120, for crochet instructions) across top of bag front, skipping every 3rd stitch or garter row, work 6 slip sts along strap, work sc as before to center of bag back, ch 20 for button loop, work sc as before to strap, work 6 slip sts along strap. Join to beg sc with a slip st. Fasten off.

Weave in loose ends.

Inspiration for bag shapes can come from unlikely places—the earflaps of a hat, for example.

PENNY RUG PURSE
MAGS KANDIS

Inspired by a photograph of a penny rug she had snipped from a catalog years ago, Mags Kandis designed this colorful boxy bag. She worked the body of the bag in one piece, from the top of the front, down to the lower edge, across the base, then back up to the top of the back—ending with the foldover flap. Mags chose a lively stripe pattern for the front and back and a contrasting but coordinating intarsia dot pattern (accented with circles of felt) for the flap. To give the bag its distinctive shape, Mags sewed gussets in the base, then felted the bag in her washing machine and blocked it over a cardboard snack box of the appropriate dimensions. The straps are narrow strips of stockinette stitch that curl naturally into rounded tubes.

STITCH GUIDE

Stripe Pattern
Work the indicated number of rows of each color in St st: 4 rows E, 2 rows G, 2 rows C, 2 rows D, 2 rows H, 2 rows A, 2 rows I, 4 rows B, 2 rows G, 2 rows F, 4 rows H, 2 rows J, 2 rows E, 2 rows C, 2 rows B, 2 rows D, 2 rows I, 4 rows A, 2 rows F, 2 rows J.
Repeat these 48 rows for pattern.

> **NOTE**
> ✦ The chart is worked in stockinette-stitch intarsia. Use a different length of yarn for each color section and twist the yarns at the color changes to prevent holes.

FINISHED SIZE
About 12½" (32 cm) wide, 14¾" (37.5 cm) tall, and 3" (7.5 cm) deep before felting; 8" (20.5 cm) wide, 7" (18 cm) tall, and 2" (5 cm) deep after felting.

YARN
Sportweight (#2 Fine).

Shown here: Brown Sheep Nature Spun Sport Weight (100% wool; 184 yd [168 m]/50 g): #880 charcoal (gray; A), #N17 French clay (orange; B), #N30 Nordic blue (medium blue; C), #155 bamboo (pale green; D), #235 beet red (wine; E), #308 sunburst gold (yellow; F), #N80 mountain purple (purple; G), #N21 mallard (teal; H), #101 burnt sienna (rust; I), and #522 nervous green (olive; J), 1 ball each.

NEEDLES
Body and strap loops—size 6 (4 mm). Strap—size 10½ (6.5mm). Adjust needle size if necessary to obtain the correct gauge.

NOTIONS
Tapestry needle; sharp-point embroidery needle with an eye large enough to accommodate yarn for French knots; scissors; net laundry bag.

GAUGE
18 stitches and 26 rows = 4" (10 cm) in stockinette stitch on smaller needles, before felting.

Penny

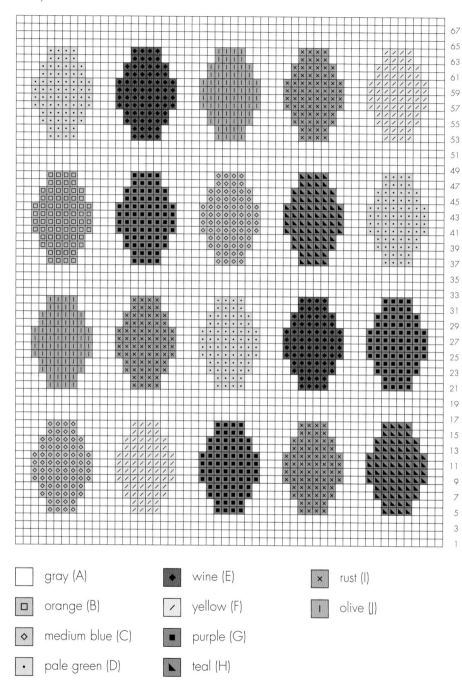

67
65
63
61
59
57
55
53
51
49
47
45
43
41
39
37
35
33
31
29
27
25
23
21
19
17
15
13
11
9
7
5
3
1

BODY

With E and smaller needles, CO 70 sts.

Front

Work stripe patt (see Stitch Guide) 2 times—96 rows total.

Base

Change to A. Work in St st for 20 rows.

Back

Change to J. Beg with 2 rows of J, work stripe patt in reverse order 2 times, ending with 4 rows of E—96 rows total for back. With E, BO 7 sts, change to A and knit to last 7 sts, change to E and BO rem 7 sts—56 sts rem. With A, purl 1 (WS) row.

Flap

Work Rows 1–68 of Penny chart. BO all sts.

STRAP LOOPS (make 2)

With smaller needles and A, CO 5 sts. Work in St st for 36 rows. BO all sts.

STRAP

With 2 strands of A held tog and larger needles, CO 5 sts. Work in St st until strap measures 60" (152.5 cm) from CO. BO all sts.

☐ gray (A)

▣ orange (B)

◇ medium blue (C)

· pale green (D)

◆ wine (E)

╱ yellow (F)

■ purple (G)

◣ teal (H)

✕ rust (I)

▮ olive (J)

STRIP FOR APPLIQUÉ

With A and smaller needles, CO 18 sts. Work in St st for 10 rows. Change to B and work in St st for 10 rows. Change to C and work in St st for 10 rows. Cont in this manner, working 10 rows of each color until all 10 colors have been used. BO all sts.

FINISHING

Weave in loose ends.

With WS facing, fold bag in half aligning stripes of front and back, and with A threaded on a tapestry needle, sew side seams. With bag inside out, flatten base so that the middle of the base is centered and faces up as described in Design Notebook (pages 106–107). With A threaded on a tapestry needle, sew across base about 2" (5 cm) from each corner. Fold corner points towards center of bag base and lightly stitch into place.

With A threaded on a tapestry needle and RS facing, attach strap loops to top of bag 7 sts from each side of seam.

Felting

Place all pieces in net laundry bag and run through washer cycle set on small load, hot wash, and cold rinse, adding a small amount of mild detergent. Stop the washer periodically to check the progress of the felting; run through additional cycles if necessary to achieve the desired amount of felting (no stitches should be visible). When pieces have felted enough, remove from washer. Pull strap and appliqué piece into shape and allow to dry flat.

To create a flat bottom, block the bag by slipping it over a plastic-wrapped box that is roughly the same size. Allow to air-dry thoroughly. Press bag and flap with warm iron, using steam as needed.

Cut and Join Appliqué Circles

With sharp scissors, cut 2 circles about ½" (1.3 cm) in diameter of each of the 10 colors—20 circles total. With contrasting yarns and using the photo as a guide, attach circles to center of round motifs on flap with French knots (see Glossary, page 121).

Adjust strap for desired length and attach to bag by folding over each strap loop and stitching firmly in place with E.

A foldover flap makes a simple closure.

Although this bag is visually complex, **Theresa Schabes** designed it to be surprisingly quick and easy to knit. She worked the rectangular front and back in a simple knit-purl pattern, then knitted a long gusset to connect them along the sides and base with a decorative whipstitch. For more embellishment, she worked a contrasting yarn through the purl bumps in an embroidery technique known as surface weaving. Theresa lined the inside of the bag and added strong suede handles sewn on with upholstery thread so that even heavy loads would be secure.

STITCH GUIDE

Pattern Stitch (multiple of 3 stitches + 2)
Row 1: (RS) Knit.
Rows 2 and 4: (WS) Purl.
Rows 3 and 5: K2, *p1, k2; rep from * to end of row.
Row 6: Purl.
Repeat Rows 1–6 for pattern.

BACK

With 1 strand of each color held tog, CO 38 sts. Rep Rows 1–6 of patt st (see Stitch Guide) until piece measures 18" (45.5 cm) from CO, ending with Row 2 of patt. BO all sts.

FRONT

CO 38 sts and work same as back.

SIDE AND BOTTOM

With 1 strand of each color held tog, CO 9 sts. Work in St st until piece measures 51" (129.5 cm) from CO, ending with a WS row. BO all sts.

FINISHING

Block pieces to measurements.

FINISHED SIZE

About 15" (38 cm) wide, 18" (45.5 cm) tall, and 3" (7.5 cm) deep.

YARN

Worsted weight (#4 Medium).

Shown here: Classic Elite Renaissance (100% wool; 110 yd [101 m]/50 g): #7127 chianti (wine), 5 balls; #7155 Renaissance red (red), #7178 tiled roof (rust), and #7185 portofino orange (orange), 3 balls each.

NEEDLES

Size 13 (9 mm). Adjust needle size if necessary to obtain the correct gauge.

NOTIONS

Tapestry needle; sharp-point sewing needle; upholstery-weight sewing thread; 24" (61 cm) brown suede handles (available at www.somersetdesigns.com); 1½ yd (1.4 m) lining fabric (optional).

GAUGE

10 stitches and 17 rows = 4" (10 cm) in pattern stitch with 4 strands of yarn held together.

Add bold texture with embroidery.

Surface Weaving

With three strands of wine threaded on a tapestry needle, weave pattern from lower edge to upper edge of bag back and front as shown below. Bring needle up between first two columns of purl bumps, two rows below the first purls. Sew a zigzag line between the purl bumps of the first two columns of purl stitches by bringing tapestry needle under first two purl bumps of first column, then under second two purl bumps of second column. Cont in this manner, bringing the tapestry needle under the next two purl bumps of the first column, then under the following two purl bumps of the second column (Figure 1), to the top of the knitted piece, being careful not to pucker the fabric. At the top, catch the yarn by going underneath the stitch that is centered between the purl columns, two rows above the last purl bumps. Turn the fabric upside down and work a zigzag line as before, using the same two purl columns to form Xs between the purl columns (Figure 2). At the end of the columns, insert the tapestry needle into the fabric to catch the yarn as before, then bring it up between the second and third purl columns. Cont in this manner until all purl columns have been worked, forming a grid of Xs. Working in rows from selvedge edge to selvedge, work a backstitch to secure each X (Figure 3).

Seams

With three strands of wine, use a whipstitch (see Glossary, page 124) to sew side and bottom piece to front and back. Whipstitch around bag opening. Weave in loose ends.

Lining (optional)

Cut two rectangles of lining fabric, each measuring 16½" x 19½" (42 x 49.5 cm), and one strip measuring 4" x 54" (10 x 137 cm). Sew pieces tog as in bag construction, using a ½" (1.3 cm) seam allowance. Fold over top edge 1" (2.5 cm) and insert inside bag with WS tog. Sew to WS of bag along top opening.

With sewing needle and matching thread, sew handles securely to front and back.

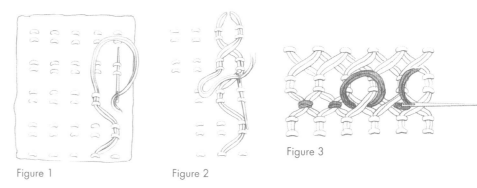

Figure 1

Figure 2

Figure 3

Sew a zigzag line between adjacent columns of purl bumps, then sew back stitches across crossed threads.

Four colors of yarn are worked together for a tweedy effect.

design**NOTEBOOK**

BAGS: VARIATIONS ON A THEME

A bag is a container for things you need to carry. It can come in many shapes and sizes. At the small end is the clutch, usually a small, flatish rectangle, designed to hold just the necessities—keys, driver's license, and lip gloss. A typical clutch is rectangular or oval and can be held in your hand or tucked under your arm. A handbag or purse is somewhat larger than a clutch and can accommodate more of your daily paraphernalia—sunglasses, cell phone, day-timer or BlackBerry—maybe even lunch—in addition to keys, wallet, and makeup. Although they can be just about any shape, handbags are often rectangular. Most handbags and purses have some type of handle or strap and a serious closure (e.g., snap, zipper) to keep valuables secure. Next up in size is the tote, usually a tall rectangular bag with an open top. Totes are great for carrying books, beach supplies, groceries, even overnight necessities. A messenger bag is a wide rectangular bag designed to carry office files, letters, and small packages. Because people who carry messenger bags often travel by bicycle, most bags of this type have a secure closure and a strap long enough to fit diagonally across the shoulders. A backpack is similar in shape to a tote, but it closes at the top and is worn on the back, held by shoulder straps.

Whether you want to make a small dressy purse or a casual book bag, the construction techniques are the same—choose a yarn, decide on a size and shape, knit or crochet the necessary pieces, assemble them, add a handle or strap, give it a closure and a bit of extra stability, if necessary, and voilà—you've got it made.

A MATTER OF SHAPE

A bag, whether flat or dimensional, can be almost any shape (as you've seen in these pages), but most are based on a square, rectangle, or circle. Fortunately, all of the basic shapes are easy to knit or crochet, leaving you free to fool around with stitch, cable, and/or color-work patterns. All you need to do is measure your gauge, decide on the size and shape, and follow the simple instructions given here.

Square or Rectangle

To knit a flat square or rectangular bag, simply cast on the number of stitches necessary for the desired width, then knit to the desired height for the front of the bag, do the same for the back of the bag, and sew the two pieces together along the base and sides. To avoid one of the seams, cast on the number of stitches for the desired width, then knit to twice the desired height, fold the fabric in half widthwise so that the fold line forms the base, and sew the bag together along the two sides. Or work the bag sideways: Cast on the number of stitches that corresponds to the desired height, knit to twice the desired width, then fold the fabric in half lengthwise so that the fold line forms one side "seam," and sew the bag together along the base and remaining side.

The process is similar for crochet—simply make a foundation chain the desired width (or height), then work to the desired height (or width).

> From a single tube of lip gloss to the week's groceries, a knitted bag can hold it all.

Circle

For a circular bag, make a circle for the front of the bag, another one for the back, and sew them together around the sides and bottom. If you're knitting, you can work the circles from the center to the outer edge. We like to use the method found in Elizabeth Zimmermann's *Knitter's Almanac* (Dover Publications, 1981) described at right. If you don't mind a few points around the outer edge of your circle, you can work your circle—from the center out or vice versa—in pie form, working increases (or decreases) along six to eight spokes. You can even work a circle shape by using short-rows. Cast on stitches to form the length of the radius of the circle. Then work short-rows to form a wedge. Work as many short-row wedges as you need to complete the circle.

If you want to crochet, a circle is best worked outward from a four- to six-stitch foundation ring. Then it's a simple matter of working in rounds and increasing stitches evenly and consistently until you reach the desired finished circumference.

Clutch

Handbag

Tote

Backpack

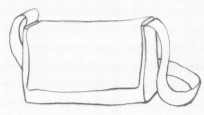

Messenger Bag

KNIT A CIRCLE À LA ELIZABETH ZIMMERMANN

With double-pointed needles, cast on 9 stitches. Join into a round and knit 1 round.

Increase Round 1: *K1, M1 (see Glossary, page 123); repeat from * to end of round—18 stitches.

Knit 3 rounds.

Increase Round 2: *K1, M1; repeat from * to end of round—36 stitches.

Knit 6 rounds.

Increase Round 3: *K1, M1; repeat from * to end of round—72 stitches.

Knit 12 rounds.

Increase Round 4: Repeat Increase Round 3—144 stitches.

Knit 24 rounds.

Continue in this manner, working twice as many knit rounds after each increase round and doubling the number of stitches in each increase round until the circle is the size you want.

Work a separate base to add depth.

THE 3-D FACTOR

Flat bags will only take you so far. They're fine for small things, but if you add a hairbrush, a book, or an apple, your bag will take on a lumpy appearance. To create more room for your belongings, you need to add a third dimension to your bag. You can add a dimension by working a separate piece (or pieces) along the bottom and/or sides or by using pleats or gathers to create more room inside.

The Base-ics

The simplest way to create a 3-D bag is to work a separate base; it can be square, rectangular, or circular—even a triangle will work. Determine the dimensions for the base, then use your gauge as a guide for the number of stitches to cast on and the number of rows to work to make the base the desired shape. If you're working a rectangular base, the long sides should represent the width of the front and back and the short ends (which will correspond to the "sides" of the bag) should measure anywhere from 1" to 6" (2.5 to 15 cm). For example, if your gauge is 5 stitches to the inch and you want the base to be 10" (25.5 cm) long and 3" (7.5 cm) deep, you can cast on 50 stitches and work 3" (7.5 cm) or you can cast on 15 stitches and work 10" (25.5 cm). Add the body either by picking up and knitting (or crocheting) stitches around the perimeter of the base or by working the body separately and sewing it to the base.

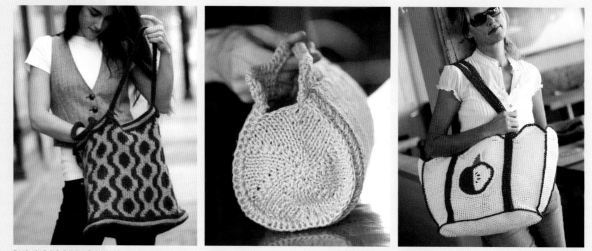

FAIR ISLE BOOK BAG | KRISTIN NICHOLAS   LINEN TUBE CLUTCH | RUTHIE NUSSBAUM   APPLE RIBBON TOTE | DRENNON/GONZALEZ

ZENITH CARPET BAG | VÉRONIK AVERY   YO-YO HOBO | JUDITH L. SWARTZ

For her Yoga Mat Tote (page 68), Sharon O'Brien knitted a square base, then picked up stitches around the edges and continued in the round for the height of the bag. You could just as easily work a rectangular base as in Kristin Nicholas's Fair Isle Book Bag (page 56), a circular one, as in Ruthie Nussbaum's Linen Tube Clutch (page 40), or an oval one, as in Bri Ana Drennon and Regina Rioux Gonzalez's Apple Ribbon Tote (page 44).

Véronik Avery modified this approach in her Zenith Carpet Bag (page 12). She worked the front and back in two separate pieces, beginning each with stitches for the base. She knitted half the depth of the base, then she cast on more stitches to extend half the width of the side gussets and knitted to the top of the bag. When she assembled the bag, she sewed the selvedge edges of the front and back base to the cast-on edges of the sides to form tidy corners.

Alternatively, you can work the entire body as a separate piece that's sewn onto the base. In her Yo-Yo Hobo (page 76), Judith L. Swartz crocheted a circle for the base, then she joined columns of crocheted medallions to the edges of the base to form the body of the bag.

The easiest way to create a 3-D bag is to work a separate base.

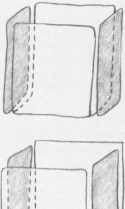

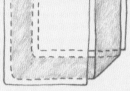

Add a separate gusset to each side or work a continuous piece that extends across the base.

Gusset Up

Many bags include a separate piece (called a gusset) that joins the front and back along the sides and base. The width of the gusset determines the depth of the bag. To make a gusset, simply decide on the width you want—from as narrow as 1" (2.5 cm) to 6" (15 cm) or wider—and, using your gauge as a guide, cast on the number of stitches that corresponds to that width. Knit the gusset for the desired length to fit around the sides and base of your bag, bind off the stitches, then sew the gusset strip to join the flat bag front and back pieces along the sides and base. To facilitate seaming, slip the first stitch of every row as you work the gusset or work the selvedge stitches in garter stitch.

For an example of gussets, see Joshua Eckels's Rugged Messenger Bag (page 26). Lisa Daehlin took the gusset "over the top" in her Lace Doily Purse (page 60), and Lisa B. Evans extended it into the shoulder strap on her Celtic Weekend Tote (page 84). For additional shaping, make the gusset wider at the base of the bag and narrower along the sides, as Mary Jane Mucklestone did for her Chullo Pouch (page 88). Consider other ways to play with gusset design: Run a cable along it, make it striped, put the seams on the outside, or work it in a different yarn or pattern stitch.

Many bags have a square or rectangular base shaped with sewn gussets. With this method, the base isn't necessarily worked as a separate piece. Instead, the base is formed by folding and stitching the knitted pieces along the bottom. To form a sewn gusset from flat pieces, sew the front and back together along the base and sides—the seams form the centerlines of base and side gussets. Then turn the bag inside out and sew (by hand or with a sewing machine) a single straight line about 1" (2.5 cm) to 3" (7.5 cm) from each corner, depending on the desired depth. Fold the corners outward toward the sides of the bag or inward toward the base of the bag and tack them in place.

RUGGED MESSENGER BAG | JOSHUA ECKELS

LACE DOILY PURSE | LISA DAEHLIN

CELTIC WEEKEND TOTE | LISA B. EVANS

CABANA BACKPACK | MAGS KANDIS   PENNY RUG PURSE | MAGS KANDIS

Mags Kandis used this type of shaping in her Cabana Backpack (page 20) as well as in her Penny Rug Purse (page 92). In both cases, she worked the front and back of the bag in a single piece that she sewed together along the sides, then she sewed across the corners to form a rectangular base and folded the corners of the gussets toward the center of the base. Norah Gaughan used similar shaping in her Classic Crocheted Purse (page 32), but she folded the corners of the gussets outward and tacked them to the side seams. Norah provided even more room inside by folding a box pleat in the center front and back of the bag. In her Felt Laptop Case (page 52), Kate Jackson worked a combination of separate gussets and pleats.

Natural Give

Sometimes you don't need (or want) to do anything special to add depth to a bag. Instead, the shape of the body or the stretch of the fabric may provide all the depth you want. Take the classic string market bag, for example. When knitted in an openwork pattern, the stitches have enough stretch to accommodate surprisingly large loads, as in Katie Himmelberg's Hemp Market Bag (page 36). Mary D'Alton worked her Two-Tone Triangle Purse (page 16) without gussets or pleats. But by shaping the bag wide at the base and leaving a broad opening at the top, the bag easily accommodates all the necessities. Pam Allen took a similar approach in her Knitting Needle Knitting Bag (page 24). The long cigar shape, wide opening, and slight gathers along the top edge allow the bag to hold a knitting project in all stages of completion, from initial cast-on to final bind-off.

Sewn Gussets

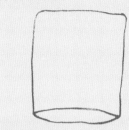

Turn the bag upside down and inside out.

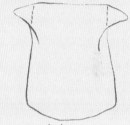

Sew a straight line across each corner.

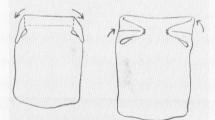

Fold and tack the corners outward to the sides or inward to the base.

Voilà—a 3-d bag!

HOLD ON

Unless a bag is small enough to hold comfortably in the palm of your hand, such as a clutch, you'll want to add some type of handle or strap. You can choose small handles that you can grasp with your hand or a long strap that rests on your shoulder. Either way, the handles or strap can be attached to the bag by continuing some of the stitches of the body or by working a separate piece (or pieces) and sewing it (or them) in place. To counteract the tendency of wool yarns to stretch, consider felting the straps or handles either in the washing machine or by hand. Or work the straps on a smaller needle, or use a "stiff" pattern stitch, such as a slip-stitch variation. Keep in mind that you're not obligated to make the straps or handles out of yarn at all—leather, nylon, metal chains, and many other materials can all be good alternatives.

Continue a Good Thing

If you design your bag with side gussets, it makes sense to continue the gusset stitches to form handles or a shoulder strap. Kate Jackson knitted a long narrow strip for the strap in her Felt Laptop Case (page 52) and sewed the ends of it to the bag front and back to form gussets, leaving a long loop in between for the shoulder strap. Lisa B. Evans extended the wide ribbed gussets (and base) of her Celtic Weekend Tote (page 84) into a comfortable strap. Mary Jane Mucklestone took a similar approach for her Chullo Pouch (page 88) by extending the stitches at the top of the gussets for the strap. For the narrow handles on her Two-Tone Triangle Purse (page 16), Mary D'Alton used the final three stitches of each "triangle" section to work a handle-length knitted cord that she sewed to the opposite side.

A handle should fit comfortably in your hand; a strap should rest comfortably on your shoulder.

CELTIC WEEKEND TOTE | LISA B. EVANS

TWO-TONE TRIANGLE PURSE | MARY D'ALTON

HEMP MARKET BAG | KATIE HIMMELBERG   LINEN TUBE CLUTCH | RUTHIE NUSSBAUM

It's also easy to pick up a few stitches from the top edge of a bag so that the handles or straps are knitted right onto the bag. For her Hemp Market Bag (page 36), Katie Himmelberg picked up a few stitches along the top of one side of the bag and knitted a long strap that she sewed securely to the top of the other side. Ruthie Nussbaum incorporated the handles in the crocheted edging of her Linen Tube Clutch (page 40) by making a hand-wide slit in the edging along the top.

Add-Ons

Of course, you can choose to work the handles or straps separately, then sew them in place. If you do, be careful to sew them securely (a backstitch seam is a good choice) so that they don't inadvertently come loose when the bag contains a heavy load.

Pam Allen worked two separate garter-stitch handles for her Knitting Needle Knitting Bag (page 24) and sewed them to the upper edge of the bag front and back. For their Apple Ribbon Tote (page 44), Bri Ana Drennon and Regina Rioux Gonzalez worked single-crochet handles long enough to sew all the way to the base of bag, thereby adding stability and structure. Lisa Daehlin took a slightly different approach with her Lace Doily Purse (page 60) by working a short double-thickness handle separately and attaching it to the bag as she worked the gusset.

For the shoulder straps in her Cabana Backpack (page 20), Mags Kandis knitted a very long and narrow stockinette-stitch strip that curled naturally into a rounded tube. She felted the rounded strap for stability, then used contrasting yarn to sew its midpoint to the center back of the bag and each end to the lower corners to provide shoulder straps. She left a few inches at each end for a final flourish—a decorative overhand knot. In her Penny Rug Purse (page 92), Mags also worked the strap as a narrow, curling stockinette-stitch strip. For strength, she gave it a good felting before sewing the ends around loops at the sides of the bag opening.

Pick up a few stitches from the top edge and knit the handle or strap right onto the bag.

Again, Mags used a bit of contrasting yarn to secure the ends. Sharon O'Brien also used the tendency of stockinette stitch to roll in on itself for the long shoulder strap of her Yoga Mat Tote (page 68). Because felting wasn't an option for Sharon's cotton yarn, she secured the rolled edges by sewing them together along the center part of the strap. She then sewed one unrolled end of the strap to the base of the bag and the other end to the top.

Kristin Nicholas decided to forego knitting and crocheting altogether and instead braided two lengths of yarn to form the straps of her Fair Isle Book Bag (page 56). She felted the braids to prevent them from stretching, then sewed them securely to the upper edge of the bag front and back. In an inventive twist of construction, Judith L. Swartz worked a single-crochet handle for her Yo-Yo Hobo (page 76), which she then attached to the bag's drawstring closure.

Something Completely Different

If you're worried about the tendency of knitted (or crocheted) stitches to stretch, consider using something other than yarn for the handles or strap. Many designers chose to use leather handles for their bags, including Norah Gaughan for her Classic Crocheted Purse (page 32), Theresa Schabes for her Surface-Woven Tote (page 96), and Véronik Avery for her Zenith Carpet Bag (page 12). Leather handles come in all shapes and sizes—check out your local craft store or the Internet for choices. If leather isn't right for your bag, try a length of nylon webbing, as Joshua Eckels did for his Rugged Messenger Bag (page 26) or a metal chain, as Laura Irwin did for her Formal Boot Bag (page 64).

Use a strong backstitch to sew handles onto a bag.

KNITTING NEEDLE KNITTING BAG | PAM ALLEN   APPLE RIBBON TOTE | DRENNON/GONZALEZ   LACE DOILY PURSE | LISA DAEHLIN

CLASSIC CROCHETED PURSE | NORAH GAUGHAN   FORMAL BOOT BAG | LAURA IRWIN

CLOSURE TIME

Once you've decided on a size, shape, and type of handle, all that's left is to add a closure to your bag—or not. From a simple overlapping flap to a zipper to a drawstring to buttons, there are many ways to make sure that valuables remain inside your bag. But depending on how your bag is constructed, you may not want (or need) any closure at all.

One of the easiest ways to keep your bag closed is to knit a flap that covers the top opening. Mags Kandis used such flaps in both her Penny Rug Purse (page 92) and Cabana Backpack (page 20). For the Penny Rug Purse, she simply knitted extra length onto the bag back (in a colorful polka-dot pattern) to extend to the base of the bag front. For her Cabana Backpack, she knitted a separate flap just big enough to cover the drawstring opening and sewed it to the top of the bag back.

A zipper makes a secure and unobtrusive closure that won't interfere with the bag design. Lisa Daehlin sewed a couple of inconspicuous zippers into the top of her Lace Doily Purse (page 60) along the seam between the front and back gussets. Joshua Eckels sewed a zipper into the top of his Rugged Messenger Bag (page 26) that's hidden by the flap overlap.

For a casual closure, use a drawstring threaded in and out of buttonholes or eyelets worked around the upper edge of the bag. For the drawstring in her Cabana Backpack (page 20), Mags Kandis worked a narrow strip, felted it, and threaded it through simple eyelets that she worked in the bag body. She then added a colorful flap to cover the drawstring. Sharon O'Brien also worked eyelets to accommodate the drawstring in her Yoga Mat Tote (page 68). In Sharon's case, she worked the drawstring in I-cord and reinforced the eyelets with contrasting crocheted circle "grommets." For her Yo-Yo Hobo (page 76), Judith L. Swartz worked spaces in the single-crocheted edging around the top of the bag to accommodate the crocheted drawstring.

Leather, nylon, metal chains, and other materials make good handles and straps.

Woven Lining

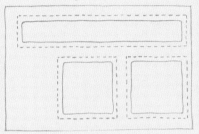

Sew the lining pieces together to match the bag shape.

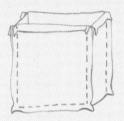

Cut pieces of lining fabric to match the knitted pieces, with extra for seam allowances.

Insert the lining inside the bag and stitch the upper edge in place.

Buttons provide simple closures that can be decorative as well as functional. For her Celtic Weekend Tote (page 84), Lisa B. Evans knitted a short tab that she sewed to the top of the bag back. She worked a buttonhole in the tab to accommodate a large wooden button sewn to the bag's front. Mary Jane Mucklestone used a single toggle button and a crocheted loop to close her Chullo Pouch (page 88).

For a sophisticated alternative to buttons, zippers, or drawstrings, consider a metal snap-frame closure as Véronik Avery did for her Zenith Carpet Bag (page 12). Snap frames are available in a variety of sizes at craft stores and the Internet. Simply sew the frame into the upper edge of the bag and let the tension of the metal hold the bag closed.

If you have trouble deciding what kind of closure to give your bag, consider no closure at all. Many bags, especially generous totes, are perfectly fine with open tops. Take Kristin Nicholas's Fair Isle Book Bag (page 56), Theresa Schabes's Surface-Woven Tote (page 96), Bri Ana Drennon and Regina Rioux Gonzalez's Apple Ribbon Tote (page 44), and Kate Jackson's Felt Laptop Case (page 52), for example. The deep shape of these bags makes it unlikely that items will fall out. Although not nearly large enough to be called a tote, Ann Budd's iPod Pocket (page 72) needs no closure because the bag stretches slightly to hold the iPod in a soft hug.

Many bags can be constructed so that the handles or straps hold the bag closed as it is carried. Good examples are Norah Gaughan's Classic Crocheted Purse (page 32), Ruthie Nussbaum's Linen Tube Clutch (page 40), Mary D'Alton's Two-Tone Triangle Purse (page 16), and Katie Himmelberg's Hemp Market Bag (page 36). These bags have a variety of shapes and sizes and a variety of handle types, but in each case, the contents are secure as soon as the bag is picked up.

YOGA MAT TOTE | SHARON O'BRIEN   **CHULLO POUCH** | MARY JANE MUCKLESTONE

YO-YO HOBO | JUDITH L. SWARTZ   ZENITH CARPET BAG | VÉRONIK AVERY

A SENSE OF STABILITY

Depending on how you plan to use your bag, you may or may not want to stabilize the stitches in some way to provide additional strength and ensure that small items don't fall out through the knitted or crocheted stitches.

Line It Up

The best way to maintain the shape and integrity of your bag, especially if it's knitted, is to line it with tightly woven fabric that will counteract the tendency of the stitches to stretch or sag. In addition, a lining gives you the opportunity to add a little extra color—anything from a wild cotton print to sophisticated silk or elegant velvet.

To line a bag, simply cut pieces of lining fabric to match the knitted bag pieces (front, back, base, and side gussets), allowing for ½" (1.3 cm) seam allowances on all sides. Sew the lining together (by hand or machine) to match the bag and turn under the seam allowance along the top edge. Insert the lining bag inside its knitted counterpart so that the wrong side of the lining faces the inside of the bag. To secure the lining in place, handstitch the upper edge to the bag. You may also want to tack the lining to the bag along the base or side seams.

For her Yo-Yo Hobo (page 76), Judith L. Swartz cut a circle of cotton fabric to match the size of the bag base and another piece to match the height and circumference of the bag body. She sewed the two pieces together to match the dimensions of the crocheted pieces and sewed them in place to the upper edge of the bag. Judith chose a color that coordinated with the warm pinks and oranges of her yarn. Véronik Avery also added a lining to her Zenith Carpet Bag (page 12), but she chose a solid-color silky fabric to match its sophisticated look.

There are lots of ways to make a knitted bag strong and secure.

BAG TIPS

✛ Add a contrasting lining for a bit of color interest.

✛ Instead of buttons, try large colorful beads.

✛ Add smooth leather handles for a dressy look.

✛ Use a noncurling stitch pattern (e.g., garter stitch, seed stitch) or a rib along the top opening, unless you plan to felt the bag.

✛ Add metal rings, buckles, and fasteners for textural contrast. You can shop for them in a sewing store or take them from finds in a secondhand store.

✛ For stability, add a lining or felt the bag to tighten up the stitches.

✛ Use stitch or color patterns or mix yarn textures for visual interest.

Feel Like Felting?

Felting is a good way to stabilize an unlined bag. If you use a yarn that contains a significant proportion of wool, you can felt the knitted bag (either by hand or in a washing machine) to tighten up the stitches and create a dense fabric. Keep in mind that felting is not reversible and that the degree of felting is influenced by water temperature, water alkalinity, amount of soap, and agitation. As you felt a project, be careful to check on the progress often to ensure even results without overfelting.

You can felt the individual bag pieces before you sew them together, as Joshua Eckels did for his Rugged Messenger Bag (page 26), or you can assemble the bag before you felt it, as Kate Jackson did for her Felt Laptop Case (page 52) and Mary D'Alton for her Two-Tone Triangle Purse (page 16). For both her Penny Rug Purse (page 92) and Cabana Backpack (page 20), Mags Kandis chose to assemble the bag body first (front, back, and base). She then felted the body, straps, and overlaps separately before sewing them all together. Laura Irwin combined felted and unfelted components to give an interesting mix of textures to her Formal Boot Bag (page 64).

Insert This

Whether or not you line or felt your bag, you may want to increase its stability and define its shape with a cardboard insert. For her Classic Crocheted Purse (page 32), Norah Gaughan used a strip of cardboard cut to the dimensions of her bag's base to reinforce its shape. She also added a lining to help stabilize the nonfelted lower portion.

TWO-TONE TRIANGLE PURSE | MARY D'ALTON PENNY RUG PURSE | MAGS KANDIS

CLASSIC CROCHETED PURSE | NORAH GAUGHAN   FAIR ISLE BOOK BAG | KRISTIN NICHOLAS   CHULLO POUCH | MARY JANE MUCKLESTONE

For a more flexible stabilizer that won't crease when bent, use plastic needlepoint canvas (available at craft stores). Kristin Nicholas lined her Fair Isle Book Bag (page 56), but she also inserted a rectangular piece of needlepoint canvas along the bottom to give the bag a firm base. To maintain the cylindrical shape of her Linen Tube Clutch (page 40), Ruthie Nussbaum inserted plastic needlepoint canvas between the knitted outer layer of the purse and the knitted lining, as well as circles against the ends.

Tighten Up
Another way to give stability to your bag is to work it at a tight gauge. Bri Ana Drennon and Regina Rioux Gonzalez's Apple Ribbon Tote (page 44) is tightly crocheted out of stiff raffia ribbon. Even without a lining or a firm insert, the bag holds its shape. Mary Jane Mucklestone used dense garter stitch for her Chullo Pouch (page 88).

Leave It Loose
Sometimes, you may intentionally avoid anything that would make your bag stiff or dense. Katie Himmelberg, for example, went for maximum flexibility in her Hemp Market Bag (page 36) and did nothing to stabilize the bag other than work the upper edge and handles in noncurling garter stitch. Because she wasn't concerned about large grocery items falling out, she chose an open stitch pattern that favors maximum stretch over density or stability.

In some cases, you may want to avoid anything that would make your bag stiff or dense.

THOSE LITTLE EXTRAS

Once you've added handles or straps, a closure, and some type of stability, take a step back and consider whether a bit of embellishment might be in order. Sometimes, embroidery, appliqué, or a few carefully placed buttons or beads can add just the right touch.

Embroidery

Embroidery is an easy way to introduce color without having to knit-in complicated Fair Isle or intarsia patterns. Sharon O'Brien embroidered colorful spirals against the solid blue background of her Yoga Mat Tote (page 68), and Kristin Nicholas punctuated the two-color knitted pattern of her Fair Isle Book Bag (page 56) with bold cross-stitches in a bright contrasting third color. It's especially easy to add embroidery to a piece that's been felted—you can insert the embroidery needle wherever you want and the embroidered stitches are less apt to distort the knitted background. Alternatively, you can follow Theresa Schabes's lead and use purl stitches to guide your embroidery, as in the Surface-Woven Tote (page 96).

Buttons, bobbles, or baubles can add sophistication or whimsy.

YOGA MAT TOTE | SHARON O'BRIEN

FAIR ISLE BOOK BAG | KRISTIN NICHOLAS

SURFACE-WOVEN TOTE | THERESA SCHABES

PENNY RUG PURSE | MAGS KANDIS   KNITTING NEEDLE KNITTING BAG | PAM ALLEN

Appliqué

For a bolder, 3-D look, try appliqué instead of embroidery, as Mags Kandis did to decorate the flaps on both her Penny Rug Purse (page 92) and Cabana Backpack (page 20). For her Penny Rug Purse, Mags knitted a striped piece of stockinette stitch, felted it, then cut out tiny circles that she sewed on top of the knitted-in circles on the flap. For her Cabana Backpack, she crocheted rings that she sewed to the flap before she felted it. Just like embroidery, appliqué is easier to attach to firm fabrics, especially ones that have been felted.

And More

There are lots of other ways to add color or texture interest to any knitted bag. Consider buttons, bows, beads, sequins, and woven-in ribbons, for just a few. Although buttons make good closures, they're also great as decorative additions. Laura Irwin used cloth-covered buttons in different sizes to accentuate the unusual silhouette she gave her Formal Boot Bag (page 64). Pam Allen turned to her wooden needle collection to add a whimsical focal point to her Knitting Needle Knitting Bag (page 24). The needles give the opening stability while also announcing the purpose of the bag.

> There are lots of ways to add color or texture interest to any knitted bag.

ABBREVIATIONS

beg	begin(s); beginning		rnd(s)	round(s)
BO	bind off		RS	right side
CC	contrast color		sl	slip
cm	centimeter(s)		sl st	slip st (slip 1 stitch purlwise unless otherwise indicated)
cn	cable needle		ssk	slip 2 stitches knitwise, one at a time, from the left needle to right needle, insert left needle tip through both front loops and knit together from this position (1 stitch decrease)
CO	cast on			
cont	continue(s); continuing			
dec(s)	decrease(s); decreasing		st(s)	stitch(es)
dpn	double-pointed needles		St st	stockinette stitch
foll	follow(s); following		tbl	through back loop
g	gram(s)		tog	together
inc(s)	increase(s); increasing		WS	wrong side
k	knit		wyb	with yarn in back
k1f&b	knit into the front and back of same stitch		wyf	with yarn in front
kwise	knitwise, as if to knit		yd	yard(s)
m	marker(s)		yo	yarnover
MC	main color		*	repeat starting point
mm	millimeter(s)		* *	repeat all instructions between asterisks
M1	make one (increase)		( )	alternate measurements and/or instructions
p	purl		[ ]	work instructions as a group a specified number of times
p1f&b	purl into front and back of same stitch			
patt(s)	pattern(s)			
psso	pass slipped stitch over			
pwise	purlwise, as if to purl			
rem	remain(s); remaining			
rep	repeat(s); repeating			
rev St st	reverse stockinette stitch			

BIND-OFFS

I-Cord Bind-Off

With right side facing and using the knitted method, cast on 3 stitches (for cord) onto the end of the needle holding the stitches to be bound off (Figure 1), *k2, k2tog through back loops (the last cord stitch with the first stitch to be bound off; Figure 2), slip these 3 stitches back to the left needle (Figure 3), and pull the yarn firmly from the back. Repeat from * until 3 stitches remain on left needle and no stitches remain on right needle. Bind off remaining stitches using the standard method.

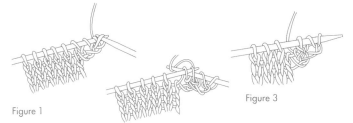

Figure 1

Figure 2

Figure 3

Standard Bind-Off

Knit the first stitch, *knit the next stitch (2 stitches on right needle), insert left needle tip into first stitch on right needle (Figure 1) and lift this stitch up and over the second stitch (Figure 2) and off the needle (Figure 3). Repeat from * for the desired number of stitches.

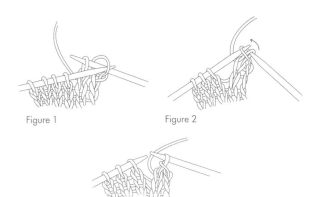

Figure 1

Figure 2

Figure 3

Three-Needle Bind-Off

Place the stitches to be joined onto two separate needles and hold the needles parallel so that the right sides of knitting face together. Insert a third needle into the first stitch on each of two needles (Figure 1) and knit them together as one stitch (Figure 2), *knit the next stitch on each needle the same way, then use the left needle tip to lift the first stitch over the second and off the needle (Figure 3). Repeat from * until no stitches remain on first two needles. Cut yarn and pull tail through last stitch to secure.

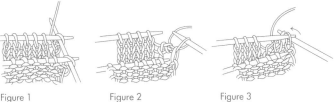

Figure 1

Figure 2

Figure 3

CAST-ONS

Backward-Loop Cast-On

*Loop working yarn and place it on needle backward so that it doesn't unwind. Repeat from *.

Figure 1

Chain-Edge Cast-On

Place a slipknot on a crochet hook. Hold the needle and yarn in your left hand with the yarn under the needle. Place hook over needle, wrap yarn around hook, and pull the loop through the slip-knot (Figure 1). *Bring yarn to back under needle, wrap yarn around hook, and pull it through loop on hook (Figure 2). Repeat from * until there is one less than the desired number of stitches. Bring the yarn to the back and slip the remaining loop from the hook onto the needle.

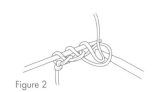

Figure 1

Figure 2

Long-Tail (Continental) Cast-On

Leaving a long tail (about ½" (1.3 cm) for each stitch to be cast on), make a slipknot and place on right needle. Place thumb and index finger of your left hand between the yarn ends so that working yarn is around your index finger and tail end is around your thumb and secure the yarn ends with your other fingers. Hold your palm upwards, making a V of yarn (Figure 1). *Bring needle up through loop on thumb (Figure 2), catch first strand around index finger, and go back down through loop on thumb (Figure 3). Drop loop off thumb and, placing thumb back in V configuration, tighten resulting stitch on needle (Figure 4). Repeat from * for the desired number of stitches.

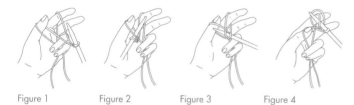

Figure 1   Figure 2   Figure 3   Figure 4

Invisible Provisional Cast-On

Make a loose slipknot of working yarn and place it on the right needle. Hold a length of contrasting waste yarn next to the slipknot and around your left thumb; hold working yarn over your left index finger. *Bring the right needle forward under waste yarn, over working yarn, grab a loop of working yarn (Figure 1), then bring needle back behind the working yarn and grab a second loop (Figure 2). Repeat from * for the desired number of stitches. When you're ready to work in the opposite direction, place the exposed loops on a knitting needle as you pull out the waste yarn.

Figure 1   Figure 2

CROCHET

Crochet Chain (ch)

Make a slipknot and place it on crochet hook if there isn't a loop already on the hook. *Yarn over hook and draw through loop on hook. Repeat from * for the desired number of stitches. To fasten off, cut yarn and draw end through last loop formed.

Double Crochet (dc)

*Yarn over hook, insert hook into a stitch, yarn over hook and draw a loop through (3 loops on hook), yarn over hook (Figure 1) and draw it through 2 loops, yarn over hook and draw it through remaining 2 loops (Figure 2). Repeat from * for the desired number of stitches.

Figure 1   Figure 2

Half Double Crochet (hdc)

*Yarn over hook, insert hook into a stitch, yarn over hook and draw a loop through (3 loops on hook), yarn over hook (Figure 1) and draw a loop through all the loops on the hook (Figure 2). Repeat from * for the desired number of stitches.

Figure 1   Figure 2

Single Crochet (sc)

*Insert hook into the second chain from the hook (or the next stitch), yarn over hook and draw through a loop, yarn over hook (Figure 1), and draw it through both loops on hook (Figure 2). Repeat from * for the desired number of stitches.

Figure 1   Figure 2

Slip-Stitch Crochet (slip st)

*Insert hook into stitch, yarn over hook and draw a loop through both the stitch and the loop already on hook. Repeat from * for the desired number of stitches.

DECREASES

Knit 2 Together (k2tog)
Knit 2 stitches together as if they were a single stitch.

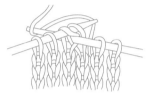

Slip, Slip, Knit (ssk)
Slip 2 stitches individually knitwise (Figure 1), insert left needle tip into the front of these 2 slipped stitches, and use the right needle to knit them together through their back loops (Figure 2).

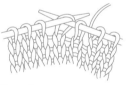

Figure 1

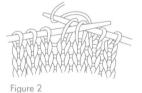

Figure 2

Slip, Slip, Slip, Knit (sssk)
Slip 3 stitches individually knitwise (Figure 1), insert left needle tip into the front of these 3 slipped stitches, and use the right needle to knit them together through their back loops (Figure 2).

Figure 1

Figure 2

EMBROIDERY

Backstitch
Bring threaded needle out from back to front between the first 2 knitted stitches you want to cover. *Insert the needle at the right edge of the right stitch to be covered, then bring it back out at the left edge of the second stitch. Insert the needle again between these 2 stitches and bring it out between the next 2 to be covered. Repeat from *.

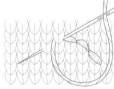

Daisy Stitch
*Bring threaded needle out of knitted background from back to front, form a short loop and insert needle into background where it came out. Keeping the loop under the needle, bring the needle back out of the background a short distance away (Figure 1), pull loop snug, and insert needle into fabric on far side of loop. Beginning each stitch at the same point in the background, repeat from * for the desired number of petals (Figure 2; 6 petals shown)

Figure 1

Figure 2

French Knot
Bring threaded needle out of knitted background from back to front, wrap yarn around needle one to three times, and use your thumb to hold the wraps in place while you insert needle into background a short distance from where it came out. Pull the needle through the wraps into the background.

Running Stitch

Bring threaded needle in and out of background to form a dashed line.

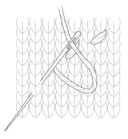

Split Stitch

Bring threaded needle from back to front, and *insert needle into a stitch a short distance to the right, then back out in the stitch to the left, piercing the center of the working thread. Repeat from *.

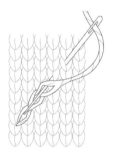

GRAFTING

Kitchener Stitch

Arrange stitches on two needles so that there is the same number of stitches on each needle. Hold the needles parallel to each other with wrong sides of the knitting together. Allowing about ½" (1.3 cm) per stitch to be grafted, thread matching yarn on a tapestry needle. Work from right to left as follows:

Step 1. Bring tapestry needle through the first stitch on the front needle as if to purl and leave the stitch on the needle (Figure 1).

Step 2. Bring tapestry needle through the first stitch on the back needle as if to knit and leave that stitch on the needle (Figure 2).

Step 3. Bring tapestry needle through the first front stitch as if to knit and slip this stitch off the needle, then bring tapestry needle through the next front stitch as if to purl and leave this stitch on the needle (Figure 3).

Step 4. Bring tapestry needle through the first back stitch as if to purl and slip this stitch off the needle, then bring tapestry needle through the next back stitch as if to knit and leave this stitch on the needle (Figure 4).

Repeat Steps 3 and 4 until 1 stitch remains on each needle, adjusting the tension to match the rest of the knitting as you go. To finish, bring tapestry needle through the front stitch as if to knit and slip this stich off the needle, then bring tapestry needle through the back stitch as if to purl and slip this stitch off the needle.

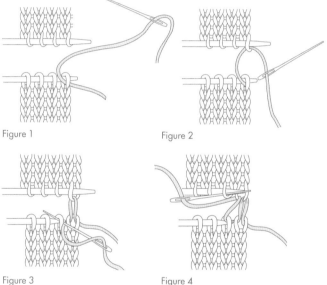

Figure 1 Figure 2

Figure 3 Figure 4

Kitchener Stitch for Ribbing

Divide the stitches on each piece between two needles—all of the knit stitches on one needle and all of the purl stitches on the other. Graft the sets of knit stitches together as described for stockinette stitch. Turn the work around so that the purl stitches appear as knit stitches and do the same. This will reduce the elasticity of the ribbing because the grafting yarn makes two passes across the piece and stitches are skipped in each pass.

INCREASES

Bar (k1f&b)

Knit into a stitch but leave it on the left needle (Figure 1), then knit through the back loop of the same stitch (Figure 2) and slip the original stitch off the needle (Figure 3).

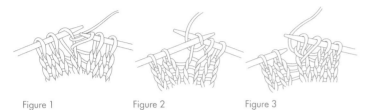

Figure 1   Figure 2   Figure 3

Raised Make One (M1)

Note: Use the left slant if no direction of slant is specified.

Left Slant (M1L): With left needle tip, lift the strand between the last knitted stitch and the first stitch on the left needle from front to back (Figure 1), then knit the lifted loop through the back (Figure 2).

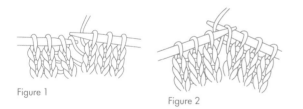

Figure 1

Figure 2

Right Slant (M1R): With left needle tip, lift the strand between the needles from back to front (Figure 1). Knit the lifted loop through the front (Figure 2).

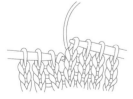

Figure 1   Figure 2

YARNOVERS

Yarnover between 2 knit stitches

Wrap the working yarn around the needle from front to back and in position to knit the next stitch.

Yarnover after a knit before a purl

Wrap the working yarn around the needle from front to back then under the needle to the front again in position to purl the next stitch.

Yarnover between 2 purl sts

Wrap the working yarn around the needle from front to back, then under the needle to the front in position to purl the next stitch.

Yarnover after purl before knit

Wrap the working yarn around the needle from front to back and in position to knit the next stitch.

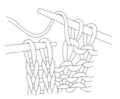

I-CORD (ALSO CALLED KNIT-CORD)

Using two double-pointed needles, cast on the desired number of stitches (usually 3 to 4). *Without turning the needle, slide stitches to other end of needle, pull the yarn around the back, and knit the stitches as usual. Repeat from * for desired length.

SEAMS

Backstitch

Pin pieces to be seamed with right sides facing together. Working from right to left into the stitch just below the bind-off row, bring threaded needle up between the first 2 stitches on each piece of knitted fabric, then back down through both layers, 1 stitch to the right of the starting point (Figure 1). *Bring the needle up through both layers a stitch to the left of the backstitch just made (Figure 2), then back down to the right, through the same hole used before (Figure 3). Repeat from *, working backward 1 stitch for every 2 stitches worked forward.

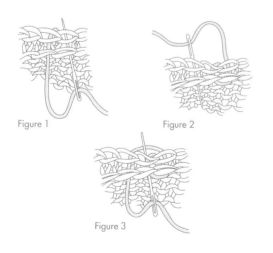

Figure 1

Figure 2

Figure 3

Mattress Stitch

Place the pieces to be seamed on a table, right sides facing up. Begin at the lower edge and work upward as foll: Insert threaded needle under one bar between the 2 edge stitches on one piece (Figure 1), then under the corresponding bar plus the bar above it on the other piece (Figure 2). *Pick up the next two bars on the first piece (Figure 3), then the next two bars on the other. Repeat from *, ending by picking up the last bar or pair of bars on the first piece.

To reduce bulk in the mattress stitch seam, work as above but pick up the bars in the center of the edge stitches instead of between the last 2 stitches.

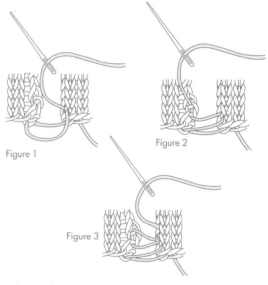

Figure 1

Figure 2

Figure 3

Whipstitch

Hold pieces to be seamed together so that the edges to be seamed are even with each other. With yarn threaded on a tapestry needle, *insert needle through both layers from back to front, then bring needle to back. Repeat from *, keeping even tension on the seaming yarn.

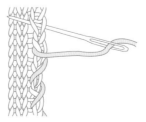

SHORT-ROWS

Knit Side

Work to turning point, slip next stitch purlwise (Figure 1), bring the yarn to the front, then slip the same stitch back to the left needle (Figure 2), turn the work around and bring the yarn in position for the next stitch—one stitch has ben wrapped and the yarn is correctly positioned to work the next stitch. When you come to a wrapped stitch on a subsequent row, hide the wrap by working it together with the wrapped stitch as follows: Insert right needle tip under the wrap (from the front if wrapped stitch is a knit stitch; from the back if wrapped stitch is a purl stitch; Figure 3), then into the stitch on the needle, and work the stitch and its wrap together as a single stitch.

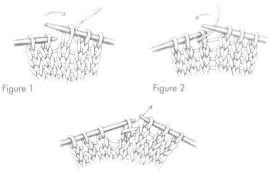

Figure 1   Figure 2

Figure 3

Purl Side

Work to the turning point, slip the next stitch purlwise to the right needle, bring the yarn to the back of the work (Figure 1), return the slipped stitch to the left needle, bring the yarn to the front between the needles (Figure 2), and turn the work so that the knit side is facing—one stitch has been wrapped and the yarn is correctly positioned to knit the next stitch. To hide the wrap on a subsequent purl row, work to the wrapped stitch, use the tip of the right needle to pick up the wrap from the back, place it on the left needle (Figure 3), then purl it together with the wrapped stitch.

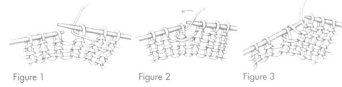

Figure 1   Figure 2   Figure 3

ZIPPER

With right side facing and zipper closed, pin zipper to knitted pieces so edges cover the zipper teeth. With contrasting thread and right side facing, baste zipper in place close to teeth (Figure 1). Turn work over and with matching sewing thread and needle, stitch outer edges of zipper to wrong side of knitting (Figure 2), being careful to follow a single column of stitches in the knitting to keep zipper straight. Turn work back to right side facing, and with matching sewing thread, sew knitted fabric close to teeth (Figure 3). Remove basting.

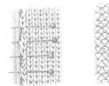

Figure 1   Figure 2   Figure 3

CONTRIBUTING DESIGNERS

Pam Allen is the creative director for Classic Elite yarns and the former editor in chief of *Interweave Knits*. She's the author of *Knitting for Dummies* and *Scarf Style*, the first book in the Style series and coauthor of *Wrap Style* and *Lace Style*.

Véronik Avery is the creative director for JCA Yarns. She has been designing knitwear for just four years and is currently working on her first book, *Knitting Classic Styles*, due out in 2007. Véronik lives in Montréal, Quebec.

Ann Budd is the former senior editor of *Interweave Knits* and is currently a book editor for Interweave Press. She is the author of *The Knitter's Handy Book* series and *Getting Started Knitting Socks* and coauthor of *Wrap Style* and *Lace Style*.

Lisa Daehlin lives in New York City, where she is an opera singer, milliner, and knitter. She teaches knitting at the Cooper Union for the Advancement of Science and Art.

Mary D'Alton is a freelance designer and stylist for commercial photography. She learned to knit in 2003 and has been enchanted with the craft ever since. She incorporates knitting into her clothing and accessory designs.

Bri Ana Drennon is a passionate fiber artist who comes from a long line of knitters, weavers, and basketmakers. A contemporary art dealer by profession, she spends her spare time crafting and blogging about all things handmade in her hometown of Los Angeles.

Joshua Eckels is the willing male mascot and second-string manager of KnitWit Yarn Shop and www.yarnonthebrain.com in Portland, Maine. Joshua really does knit and his wife, Anna, taught him everything she knows, so it's okay to ask the man behind the counter for help.

Lisa B. Evans is a landscape architect, devoted knitter, and mother of three. Involved in knitwear design for more than fifteen years, she founded LB Evans Handknits in 2001, an innovative line of knitted handbags, backpacks, and totes, which is now represented by Westminster Fibers, Inc. Lisa is also coauthor of *Hip Graphic Knits*.

Norah Gaughan is the design director for Berroco Yarns and author of *Knitting Nature: 39 Designs Inspired by Patterns in Nature*. Many of her designs highlight a simple shape with an organically influenced focal point.

Regina Rioux Gonzalez is an exhibiting artist and designer with a master's degree in fine art. She has taught fine art at the primary, secondary, and university levels. She spends her spare time transforming yarn into intriguing objects and wacky wearables.

Katie Himmelberg loves working with natural fibers and organic shapes. She is on the editorial staff of *Interweave Knits* and *Knitscene* magazines. When she's not knitting, she's probably sewing, making jewelry, cooking vegan meals, or frolicking in the nearby Rocky Mountains.

Laura Irwin lives in Portland, Oregon, where she designs knitwear for boutiques that specialize in local and independent fashion design. Her knitwear has been featured in *Venus Magazine*, and her patterns for handknits have appeared in *Knitscene* and *Interweave Knits*. Visit her blog at www.preciousknit.blogspot.com.

Kate Jackson manages, designs, and teaches classes at Knitting on the Square in Chardon, Ohio. She received a bachelor's degree in fashion design from Kent State University in 2006 and has contributed designs to several national magazines and yarn companies.

Mags Kandis's love of travel (often only "armchair"), color, culture, texture, and discovery fuels her unique and identifiable knit designs. Mags is the head designer and consultant for Mission Falls Yarns.

Mary Jane Mucklestone studied textiles and surface design from an early age and eventually earned a BFA in printmaking from Pratt Institute. She likes to work with color and enjoys the process as much as the finished items.

Kristin Nicholas is a knitwear and stitchery author and designer who lives in the wilds of western Massachusetts. She and her husband and daughter raise a large flock of sheep, pigs, exotic chickens, border collies, and farm cats. Visit her website at www.kristinnicholas.com.

Ruthie Nussbaum learned to knit as a teenager from her grandmother. She now lives in New York City, where she's a reading teacher, knitting instructor, and burgeoning knitwear designer. See more of her work at www.ruthieknits.com.

Sharon O'Brien is a self-taught knitter. She designs knitwear for national magazines and swatches for the fashion industry. Sharon teaches knitting and crochet classes at a community college near Baltimore, Maryland.

Theresa Schabes, at her mother's insistence, was knitting mittens without a pattern by age eight. She now lives in Hinsdale, Illinois, teaches knitting classes at Knitche in Downer's Grove, and runs a knitting club at her children's elementary school.

Judith L. Swartz is the author of *Dogs in Knits, Hip to Knit, Hip to Crochet,* and *Getting Started Crochet*. She lives in Spring Green, Wisconsin, where she and her husband are fourth-generation owners of a small department store with, of course, an extensive yarn department.

BERROCO INC.
PO Box 367
14 Elmdale Rd.
Uxbridge, MA 01569
www.berroco.com
In Canada: S. R. Kertzer Ltd.

BROWN SHEEP COMPANY
100662 County Rd. 16
Mitchell, NE 69357
www.brownsheep.com

CASCADE YARNS
PO Box 58168
1224 Andover Park East
Tukwila, WA 98188
www.cascadeyarns.com

CLASSIC ELITE YARNS
122 Western Ave.
Lowell, MA 01851
www.classiceliteyarns.com

DALE OF NORWAY
N16 W23390 Stone Ridge Dr., Ste. A
Waukesha, WI 53188
www.dale.no

DIAMOND YARN
9697 St. Laurent, Ste. 101
Montreal, QC
Canada H3L 2N1
and
115 Martin Ross, Unit 3
Toronto, ON
Canada M3J 2L9
www.diamondyarn.com

HARRISVILLE DESIGNS
Center Village
PO Box 806
Harrisville, NH 03450
www.harrisville.com

JCA INC./REYNOLDS
35 Scales Ln.
Townsend, MA 01469
www.jcacrafts.com

LANAKNITS DESIGNS
HEMP FOR KNITTING
320 Vernon St., Ste. 3B
Nelson, BC
Canada V1L 4E4
www.lanaknits.com

LOUET NORTH AMERICA
808 Commerce Park Dr.
Ogdensburg, NY 13669
www.louet.com
In Canada:
3425 Hands Rd.
Prescott, ON
Canada K0E 1T0

MUENCH YARNS INC./GGH
1323 Scott St.
Petaluma, CA 94954-1135
www.muenchyarns.com
In Canada: Oberlyn Yarns

OBERLYN YARNS
5640 Rue Valcourt
Brossard, QC
Canada J4W 1C5
www.oberlyn.ca

PLYMOUTH YARN CO.
500 Lafayette St.
Bristol, PA 19007
www.plymouthyarn.com

PRITCHARD PACKAGING INC.
52 Antares Dr., Unit #7
Nepean, ON
Canada K2E 7Z1
www.pritchard.com

SKACEL
PO Box 88110
Seattle, WA 98138
www.skacelknitting.com

S.R. KERTZER LTD.
50 Trowers Rd.
Woodbridge, ON
Canada L4L 7K6
www.kertzer.com

TAHKI/STACY CHARLES INC.
70–30 80th St., Bldg. 36
Ridgewood, NY 11385
www.tahkistacycharles.com
In Canada: Diamond Yarn

VERMONT ORGANIC FIBER COMPANY
52 Seymour St., Ste. 8
Middlebury, VT 05753
www.vtorganicfiber.com

WESTMINSTER FIBERS/
NASHUA HANDKNITS
165 Ledge St.
Nashua, NH 03060
www.westminsterfibers.com
In Canada: Diamond Yarn

For more knitting patterns and techniques, join the community at knittingdaily.com—where life meets knitting, or subscribe to Interweave's magazine *Interweave Knits* or *Interweave Crochet*.

knittingdaily 🧶

Join the *Bag Style* Knitalong! Share your finished objects, helpful tips, and ideas for variations on patterns from the book at www.bagstylebook.com

INDEX